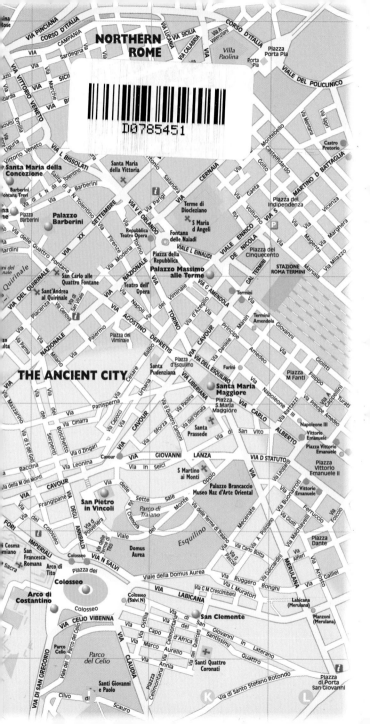

CITYPACK TOP 25
Rome

TIM JEPSON

If you have any comments
or suggestions for this guide
you can contact the editor at
Citypack@theAA.com

AA Publishing
Find out more about AA Publishing and the wide
range of services the AA provides by visiting our
website at www.theAA.com/travel

How to Use
This Book

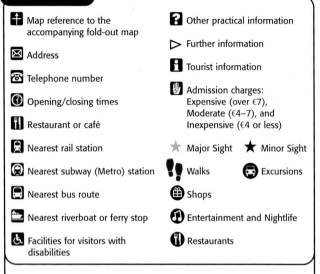

KEY TO SYMBOLS

➕ Map reference to the accompanying fold-out map

✉ Address

☎ Telephone number

🕐 Opening/closing times

🍴 Restaurant or café

🚆 Nearest rail station

Ⓜ Nearest subway (Metro) station

🚌 Nearest bus route

⛴ Nearest riverboat or ferry stop

♿ Facilities for visitors with disabilities

❓ Other practical information

▷ Further information

ℹ Tourist information

✋ Admission charges:
Expensive (over €7),
Moderate (€4–7), and
Inexpensive (€4 or less)

★ Major Sight   ★ Minor Sight

👣 Walks   🚍 Excursions

🏬 Shops

🎭 Entertainment and Nightlife

🍽 Restaurants

This guide is divided into four sections

• **Essential Rome:** an introduction to the city and tips on making the most of your stay.

• **Rome by Area:** We've broken the city into six areas, and recommended the best sights, shops, entertainment venues, nightlife and restaurants in each one. Suggested walks help you to explore on foot.

• **Where to Stay:** the best hotels, whether you're looking for luxury, budget or something in between.

• **Need to Know:** the info you need to make your trip run smoothly, including getting about by public transport, weather tips, emergency phone numbers and useful websites.

Navigation In the Rome by Area chapter, we've given each area its own colour, which is also used on the locator maps throughout the book and the map on the inside front cover.

Maps The fold-out map accompanying this book is a comprehensive street plan of Rome. The grid on this fold-out map is the same as the grid on the locator maps within the book. We've given grid references within the book for each sight and listing.

Contents

CONTENTS

Introducing Rome

Rome is one of the world's great cities, the city of the Caesars, of romance and *la dolce vita*, of long, hot sunny days, of endless art galleries, churches and museums, of fountain-splashed piazzas and majestic monuments to its golden age of empire.

It is also a city with all the myriad pleasures of any Italian destination—notably superb food and wine—as well as great bars, cafés, and shopping, vibrant nightlife and numerous cultural events. At the same time, Rome is very much a contemporary city—traffic rumbles around medieval cobbled streets and the skyline bristles not with glittering skyscrapers but with the domes of churches and palaces.

But how to visit a city where there is so much to see? First of all don't rush to the Colosseum, St. Peter's or the Sistine Chapel on your first morning. Rome for much of the year is hot and crowded. If you try to cram in too much, or soldier on through the heat, the chances are you'll emerge battered rather than enraptured. Instead, start with a stroll around the Ghetto or Trastevere, two of the city's quaintest old quarters, or

have a cappuccino in one of Rome's loveliest squares, Campo de' Fiori or Piazza Navona. Or maybe head for one of the lesser-known art-filled churches, such as Santa Maria del Popolo, crammed with masterpieces by Raphael, Pinturicchio and Caravaggio.

Once gently acclimatized, and hopefully charmed by the city's quieter side, then you can begin to think about the Trevi Fountain, the Spanish Steps, the Roman Forum or the Vatican Museums. And, of course, the newer but still relatively unsung museums that have opened in the last decade—notably the Palazzo Altemps and Palazzo Massimo alle Terme. But bear in mind this is a living city with over 3,000 years of history. One, two, even ten visits aren't enough to do it justice. However much you see, one thing for certain, you'll be back.

Facts + Figures

- **Population in 2003: 2,810,931.**
- **The official age of Rome in 2007 is 2,760 years.**
- **There have been 169 popes and 73 emperors.**
- **The area of the city covers 1,494sq km (577sq miles).**

SECRET KEYHOLE

Rome's most charming view is from Piazza dei Cavalieri di Malta on Aventine Hill. To find it, go to the left of the church of Santa Sabina and to the end of the piazza; look through the keyhole of the door (No. 3) of the Priory of the Knights of Malta. Through this tiny hole you will see a secret garden and an avenue of trees framing… but let's not spoil the surprise: see for yourself.

WATERY WASTE

More than 50 of Rome's fountains are fed by the waters of the Aqua Virgo, a source that the Romans first brought into the city in 19BC. It flows from the country-side outside the city, and feeds the Barcaccia fountain at the foot of the Spanish Steps, before supplying many others, including the most famous of them all, the Fontana di Trevi.

SWISS GUARD

The pope's official bodyguards are recruited from Switzerland's four predominantly Catholic cantons. Each must be between 19 and 25, at least 1.75cm (5ft 8in) tall and remain unmarried during their tour of duty. Their distinctive uniforms were designed by Michelangelo in the colours of the Medici popes—red, yellow and blue.

A Short Stay in Rome

DAY 1

Morning Take breakfast in a café in **Campo de' Fiori** (▷ 48), a pretty square whose market makes a lively start to the day. Then glance at Piazza Farnese before walking east through the quiet streets of the Ghetto to Piazza Venezia and up the ramp to **Piazza del Campidoglio** (▷ 34).

Mid-morning Look around the piazza, dipping into the church of **Santa Maria in Aracoeli** (▷ 35) and the **Musei Capitolini** (▷ 28–29). Or make straight for the **Foro Romano** (▷ 26–27), the **Palatino** (▷ 34) and the **Colosseum** (▷ 24–25)—take the alley and steps to the rear left of Piazza del Campidoglio for a wonderful view of the Forum.

Lunch There are several restaurants near the Colosseum, notably **Nerone** and **Pasquilino** (▷ 38). Alternatively, buy a snack in **Cavour 313** (▷ 37) or the café at the Monumento a Vittorio Emanuele II—it has great views over the Foro Romano and **Fori Imperiali** (▷ 33).

Afternoon Visit the **Palazzo Doria Pamphilj** (▷ 44–45) and see the **Colonna di Marco Aurelio** (▷ 51) before walking to the **Fontana di Trevi** (▷ 78). Then walk to **Piazza di Spagna** for the Spanish Steps (▷ 81). If you want to shop, now is the time to do so, for the streets on and around nearby Via Condotti contain Rome's best stores. If not, and you want more culture, take a short walk east to the **Palazzo Barberini** (▷ 80), passing **Santa Maria delle Concezione** (▷ 87) on the way.

Dinner Take a bus or taxi to Trastevere, which has a wide choice of places to eat (▷ 73–74).

Evening Trastevere is not the cutting-edge nightlife district it once was, but its streets remain some of Rome's prettiest places to wander after dark.

DAY 2

Morning Today explore central Rome and the **Vatican** (▷ 96–97). If you want to do the museums justice, and beat some of the crowds, you'll need at least a morning and may wish to start the day there—or save them for another, longer visit. Otherwise, have breakfast in **Piazza Navona** (▷ 49) Rome's grandest square (or in **Bar della Pace**, ▷ 58, just off it), before the crowds arrive. Then walk east to the **Pantheon** (▷ 46–47) via San Luigi dei Francesi, also seeing **Santa Maria sopra Minerva** (▷ 50).

Mid-morning Take a coffee in **La Tazza d'Oro** (▷ 60). Then walk down Via delle Coppelle to see **Sant'Agostino** (▷ 52) and the superb **Palazzo Altemps** (▷ 42–43). Walk back towards Piazza Navona and explore Via dei Coronari and/or Via del Governo Vecchio or Via dei Banchi Nuovi, three of central Rome's most interesting streets.

Lunch The streets around Piazza Navona have plenty of bars and restaurants for lunch or a snack.

Afternoon Depending on time, and whether you want to see the Vatican museums, visit the **Castel Sant'Angelo** (▷ 95). Then make for the museums, or, for a more leisurely time, confine yourself to **St. Peter's** (▷ 94).

Dinner The area around St. Peter's is not great for dining, so take the 64 bus back to the heart of the city. The streets around Piazza Navona and Campo de' Fiori have plenty of restaurants.

Evening Join the throng in Piazza Navona, indulging in a famous *tartufo* ice cream from **Tre Scalini** (▷ 60). Or have a drink in one of the area's many bars. For peace and quiet, walk east to the **Ghetto** (▷ 67), whose streets are often deserted, despite being minutes from the night-time hubbub.

ESSENTIAL ROME A SHORT STAY IN ROME

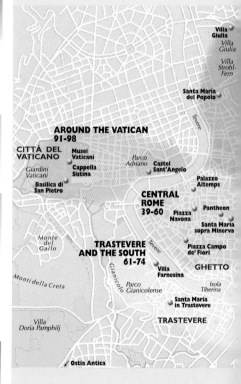
► ► ►

Basilica di San Pietro
▷ 94 Roman Catholic
Church's principal shrine
and the spiritual focus
of believers.

Castel Sant'Angelo
▷ 95 A museum that was
formerly a mausoleum and
a fortress.

Colosseo ▷ 24–25
The largest surviving
ancient Roman structure
in the world.

Villa Giulia ▷ 85
Splendidly housed in the
Villa Giulia is the National
Etruscan Museum.

Villa Farnesina ▷ 66
Peace and tranquillity away
from the city noise set in
lovely surroundings.

**Santa Maria sopra
Minerva** ▷ 50 A touch of
Gothic amid Rome's prevail-
ing Renaissance and
baroque architecture.

Santa Maria Maggiore
▷ 32 Contains the city's
highest bell tower and features a sumptuous interior.

**Santa Maria in
Trastevere** ▷ 64–65 A
rare medieval church on the
right bank of the River Tiber.

Santa Maria del Popolo
▷ 84 A must for art lovers,
with works from some of
the great names.

**San Giovanni in
Laterano** ▷ 31 Grandiose
basilica rich in interior decoration and works of art.

San Clemente ▷ 30
Remains of a temple to the
Persian god Mithras with
splendid mosaics.

Piazza Navona ▷ 49
A superb baroque city space
and the setting for three
magnificent fountains.

These pages are a quick guide to the Top 25, which are described in more detail later. Here they are listed alphabetically and the tinted background shows which area they are in.

Fontana di Trevi ▷ 78
Nicola Salvi's baroque masterpiece and Rome's most popular fountain.

Foro Romano ▷ 26–27
The heart of ancient Rome and one of the city's most evocative sites.

Museo e Galleria Borghese ▷ 79 Beloved museum with great art in beautiful surroundings.

Musei Capitolini ▷ 28–29 The oldest collection in the world, with over 1,300 works.

Musei Vaticani & Cappella Sistina ▷ 96–97 Supreme treasures spanning more than 3,000 years.

Ostia Antica ▷ 102–103 Ancient ruins, pine trees and wild spring flowers make the perfect setting.

Palazzo Altemps ▷ 42–43 A superb Renaissance building with top-class Classical sculpture.

Palazzo Barberini ▷ 80 Beautiful piazza named after the powerful Barberini family.

Palazzo-Galleria Doria Pamphilj ▷ 44–45 An important art collection displayed in a beautiful palace.

Palazzo Massimo alle Terme ▷ 82–83 Some of Rome's most magnificent Classical treasures.

NORTHERN ROME 75-90

Bioparco

Villa Paganini

Villa Albani

Villa Torlonia

Museo e Galleria Borghese

SALARIO

Villa Borghese

ncio

Galoppatoio

Villa Paolina

Piazza di Spagna

Palazzo Barberini

Giardini del Quirinale

Palazzo Massimo alle Terme

ontana di Trevi

Quirinale

Palazzo-Galleria Doria Pamphilj

Santa Maria Maggiore

olino Musei Capitolini

Parco di Traiano

Esquilino

Foro Romano

Colosseo

San Clemente

Villa Wolkonsky

Orti Farnesiani Palatino

Parco del Celio

San Giovanni in Laterano

Parco nt'Alessio

AVENTINO HILL

Villa Celimontana

THE ANCIENT CITY 21-38

Celi

ESSENTIAL ROME TOP 25

Piazza di Spagna ▷ 81
Site of the city's most stunning stairway, the Spanish Steps.

Piazza Campo de 'Fiori ▷ 48 A picturesque and atmospheric square in the heart of the city.

Pantheon ▷ 46–47 The best-preserved building from the Roman world; the last resting place of Raphael.

◀ ◀ ◀

Shopping

Rome was once the market place of an empire that embraced much of the known world. These days it has a more humble place in the shopping firmament. This said, all the great Italian retail staples—food, wine, fashion, shoes, leatherware and clothing—are well represented, and the city is a good source of art, antiques, traditional crafts and artisan products such as furniture.

More for your Money

Mid-price shoes and clothes represent good value for money; you will find them in countless shops around the new city, but particularly Via Nazionale, Via del Tritone and Via del Corso. The same streets are also dotted with small specialist shops selling good-quality bags, gloves and other leatherware. The sprawling market in an ex-barracks near Piazza Vittorio Emanuele II, where most Romans do their shopping, is also a good source of clothes and shoes, as well as pots, pans and kitchenware with an Italian stamp (such as coffee makers). In stylish Rome, even inexpensive clothes tend to be good quality and well-cut.

Designer Names

At the other sartorial extreme, most of the great Italian and European fashion houses have shops in the city: Gucci, Prada, Armani are all here, mostly in the grid of streets around Via

---

ANTIQUES

It is no wonder, given Rome's long history, that the city is a treasury of antiques. Prices are often high, but the range of objects—Etruscan, Roman, Renaissance, baroque and other items—is unrivalled. For paintings and prints, head for Via Margutta, which also has a scattering of galleries selling contemporary art and carpets, while for general antiques try Via Giulia, Via del Babuino (particularly for Persian carpets), Via dei Coronari, Via dell'Orso and Via del Monserrato. Also good, and with lower prices and less exclusive stock, are Via del Panico, Via del Pellegrino and Via dei Banchi Nuovi.

Great fashion houses sit side by side on Via Condotti, with the occasional gelaterie in between for refreshment

Condotti, an excellent source of high-class clothes, shoes, lingerie and accessories. Department stores have not really caught on, and only Coin and Rinascente are worth a visit.

Tempt your Taste Buds

Shopping for food has a unique charm in Rome, whether in the small area shops known as *alimentari*, or the specialist delicatessens in streets such as Via della Croce. The city's ancient markets, particularly Campo de' Fiori, are colourful sources of provisions. Pasta in every shape and size, the finest extra virgin oil, *funghi porcini* (dried cep mushrooms), truffle oil and spices made good food buys.

Catholic Paraphernalia

The range of shops selling ecclesiastical items is vast. The largest concentration is around St. Peter's—look out for ceramic Swiss Guards and fluorescent rosaries. On Via dei Cestari all manner of ecclesiastic garb is available—if you ever daydreamed about buying a bishop's robe or a cardinal's hat, this is the place.

Fun for the Tourist

Rome has any number of shops and stalls selling plaster and plastic casts of famous statues. Around the tourist traps are plenty of souvenirs, from figures of gladiators to models of the Colosseum. Better-quality items, plus books, prints and artistic replicas, are sold in museum and gallery shops.

Something to take home—a culinary delight, a designer bag or an exclusive little number from a top name

---

MARBLED PAPER

Notebooks and other stationery items covered with marbled paper make wonderful souvenirs, which you can find in shops all over the city. The paper originated in Venice, where the technique arrived from the East in the 15th century, and is still handmade. The process involves floating multicolour pigments on liquid gum and combing the different colours, separated by ox-gall, into distinctive patterns. The paper is placed delicately on top, then lifted and hung up to dry.

Shopping by Theme

Whether you're looking for a department store, a quirky boutique, or something in between, you'll find it all in Rome. On this page shops are listed by theme. For a more detailed write-up, see the individual listings in Rome by Area.

ACCESSORIES AND LEATHER GOODS

Gucci (▷ 89)
Mondello Ottica (▷ 56)
La Perla (▷ 89)
Sergio di Cori (▷ 89)

BOOKS AND STATIONERY

Almost Corner Bookshop
  (▷ 71)
Antica Libreria Croce
  (▷ 55)
Feltrinelli (▷ 55)
Pineider (▷ 89)
Poggi (▷ 56)
Il Sigillo (▷ 56)

DEPARTMENT STORES

Coin (▷ 37)

INTERIORS

Almaxxura (▷ 71)
Bassetti (▷ 55)
Casimon (▷ 71)
Culti (▷ 55)
Ginori (▷ 89)
House & Kitchen (▷ 56)
Lumières (▷ 71)
Maria Grazia Luffarelli
  (▷ 56)
Ornamentum (▷ 56)
Pandora (▷ 71)
Spazio Sette (▷ 56)

FOOD AND WINE

Antica Enoteca (▷ 89)
Al Monasteri (▷ 55)
Bottega del Cioccolata
  (▷ 37)
Castroni (▷ 98)
Enoteca al Goccetto
  (▷ 55)
Panella (▷ 37)
Pietro Franchi (▷ 98)
La Renella (▷ 71)

FOOTWEAR

AVC di Adriana Campanile
  (▷ 89)
Fausto Santini (▷ 89)
Ferragamo (▷ 89)

MEN'S FASHION

Battistoni (▷ 89)
Ermenegildo Zegna
  (▷ 89)
Prada (▷ 89)

OUTDOOR MARKETS

Campo de' Fiori (▷ 55)
Mercato Andrea Doria
  (▷ 98)
Mercato di Via Sannio
  (▷ 37)
Piazza Coppelle (▷ 56)
Piazza San Cosimato
  (▷ 71)
Porta Portese (▷ 71)

WOMEN'S FASHION

Ethic (▷ 55)
Fabindia (▷ 55)
Giorgio Armani (▷ 89)
Marella (▷ 89)
Prada ▷ (89)

Rome by Night

After dark the heat of a summer day gives way to balmy evenings and life takes to the streets, allowing you to share in the soft, sweet blandishments of *la dolce vita,* still as vibrant and seductive as in the heady 1950s. Bars and cafés fill with Romans at their sleek and well-dressed best, while Lotharios and lean-limbed starlets and wannabes glide around the city on snarling Vespas and in open-topped sports cars.

Roman Illuminations

The Pantheon and Colosseum are spectacular under floodlights and romantic under moonlight. St. Peter's takes on a different hue under Rome's velvety night skies—come at midnight or later and you may well have Piazza San Pietro to yourself. The experience is magical. Much the same can be said of Rome's other great set-pieces, Piazza Navona, the Trevi Fountain and Spanish Steps. Piazza Navona, like a great nocturnal salon, fills with street performers, food stalls, artists and locals and visitors there to see and be seen.

Under the Stars

If you prefer tranquillity then walk from one sleepy fountain-splashed piazza to the next, sip an aperitif in a flower-decked terrace or eat alfresco—one of Rome's pleasures. Alternatively, take in an open-air concert amid ancient Roman ruins or a beautiful Renaissance garden.

NOCTURNAL STROLLS

Rome's trendiest after-dark areas are San Lorenzo, a student and working-class district east of the city, and working-class Testaccio, to the south. Both are some way from the heart of town. So if you don't need to be at the cutting edge, spend the night in Trastevere, an established area full of small squares and pretty streets. To escape its crowds, walk to the Pincio from the top of the Spanish Steps for great sunset views, or wander through the old Ghetto area south of Via delle Botteghe Oscure, beautifully deserted after dark.

As night falls, and you move from café to bar, enjoy the city's illuminated sights along the way

Eating Out

In Rome prepare yourself for rich, sun-drenched tastes. Thousands of restaurants cater to every budget and provide every kind of dining experience. Eating is so much a social way of life that it is quite normal to spend several hours over a meal.

When to Eat
If you are eating breakfast in a bar, as many Romans do, you will find that most bars open at around 7–7.30am for cappuccino and a crois-sant. In hotels, breakfast usually starts at 8am, and includes cereal, cold meat and cheeses. Restaurants open for lunch at 12.30 or 1pm, and serve until about 3pm. Romans generally eat dinner late, so many restaurants don't open for evening meals until 8pm, although you will find some that open earlier. Many places, espe-cially cafés and bars, stay open all day.

Where to Eat
There are several different types of eating establishments in Rome. A *ristorante* tends to be the most expensive, with pristine table linen and waiters. The *trattoria* is less formal, less expensive and often family-run. An *osteria* or *hostaria* can be basic, sometimes with paper tablecloths and no written menu, but can serve some of the best food. A *rosticceria* or *tavola calda* is a fast-food outlet serving mostly cold foods. If you want pizza, look for the sign *pizzeria forno a legno* to make sure that it is traditionally cooked in a wood-fired oven.

PRICE MATTERS

Although in theory restaurants are no longer allowed to add a bread and cover charge, many feign oblivion to this and just charge for the bread anyway. Normally service is not included, although a minority of establishments do still add it as a fixed item. In everyday pizzerias, a tip of 5 per cent is perfectly adequate, but in *ristoranti*, if the service has been good, 10 per cent would be acceptable. You should always be given a receipt after paying the bill as the restaurant could be fined if they don't issue one.

Pizza, pasta or something more substantial, whatever your choice, finish it off with an espresso coffee

Restaurants by Cuisine

There are restaurants to suit all tastes and budgets in Rome. On this page they are listed by cuisine. For a more detailed description of each restaurant, see Rome by Area.

BARS BY DAY

Antica Birreria Fratelli Tempe Ra (▷ 58)
Bar della Pace (▷ 58)
Gran Caffé Martini e Rossi (▷ 38)
Latteria del Gallo (▷ 59–60)
Sacchetti (▷ 74)
Salotto 42 (▷ 60)
San Clemente (▷ 38)

COFFEE/PASTRIES

Antico Caffè Brasile (▷ 38)
Babington's Tea Rooms (▷ 90)
Bibli (▷ 73)
Caffè Farnese (▷ 58)
Sant' Eustachio (▷ 60)
La Tazza d'Oro (▷ 60)
Trastè (▷ 74)

FINE DINING

Bramante (▷ 58)
Checchino dal 1887 (▷ 73)
Il Convivio (▷ 58)
Sabatini (▷ 74)
Vecchia Roma (▷ 60)

FISH/SEAFOOD

Alberto Ciarla (▷ 73)
Dur Filettaro a Santa Barbara (▷ 59)
La Rosetta (▷ 60)

GELATERIE

Alberto Pica (▷ 73)
Da Mirella (▷ 73)
Gelateria della Palma (▷ 59)
Giolitti (▷ 59)
Tre Scalini (▷ 60)

PIZZA/PASTA

Baffetto (▷ 58)
Corallo (▷ 58)
Dar Poeta (▷ 73)
Da Vittorio (▷ 73)
Est! Est! Est! (▷ 90)
Ivo (▷ 74)
Leoncino (▷ 90)
Panattoni (▷ 74)
Pizza Ciro (▷ 90)

ROMAN/ITALIAN

Adriano (▷ 106)
Agate e Romeo (▷ 38)
Augusto (▷ 73)
Il Bacaro (▷ 58)
Borgo Nuovo (▷ 98)
Cacciani (▷ 106)
Ciccia Bomba (▷ 59)
Da Francesco (▷ 59)
Dal Toscano (▷ 98)
Ditirambo (▷ 59)
Grappolo d'Oro (▷ 59)
Il Grottino della Sibil la dal 1826 (▷ 106)
'Gusto (▷ 59)
Nerone (▷ 38)
Paris (▷ 74)
Pasquilino (▷ 38)
Sora Lella (▷ 74)
Taverna Angelica (▷ 98)
Tucci (▷ 60)
Zarazzà (▷ 106)

WORLD CUISINES

Charly's Saucière (▷ 38)
Giggetto (▷ 73)
Hasekura (▷ 38)
L'Eau Vive (▷ 60)
Piperno (▷ 74)
Thien Kim (▷ 60)
Zen Sushi (▷ 98)

If You Like...

However you'd like to spend your time in Rome, these top suggestions should help you tailor your ideal visit. Each sight or listing has a fuller write-up in Rome by Area.

BURNING THE MIDNIGHT OIL

Sit up late with the beautiful people in Bar della Pace (▷ 58).
Share a glass or two of wine with the characters in the bars around Campo de' Fiori (▷ 48).
Visit one or more of the many clubs in the Testaccio (▷ 72) nightlife district.

THE LAP OF LUXURY

Go mad in the chic designer stores in the streets around Via dei Condotti (▷ 89).
Stay in one of the city's opulent five-star hotels, notably the Hassler (▷ 112).
Eat at Convivio or La Rosetta (▷ 58, 60), two of the city's best restaurants.

Cafés in Campo dei Fiori buzz at night (top). Spoil yourself and stay in one of Rome's top hotels (above)

TO KEEP YOUR CHILDREN HAPPY

Take them to the Bioparco in the Villa Borghese (▷ 87).
Buy lots of ice cream, especially from Giolitti or Gelateria della Palma (▷ 59).
Introduce them to the characters dressed as centurions and gladiators outside the Colosseum (▷ 24–25).

SAVING FOR A RAINY DAY

Buy an integrated travel pass (▷ 118–119) and save on public transport.
Visit Rome's art-crammed churches— such as Santa Maria sopra Minerva (▷ 50)—they are virtually all free.
Time your visit for the last Sunday of the month, when the normally expensive Vatican museums (▷ 96–97) are free.

Posing outside the Colosseum (above right). Visit Santa Prassede for free (right)

A night of jazz (below). A hotel offering unparalleled views of the city (below middle)

AN EVENING OF ENTERTAINMENT

See what's playing at the Teatro dell'Opera di Roma (▷ 90).

Enjoy a night of blues or jazz at Big Mama's (▷ 72).

Look out for posters advertising church recitals and other classical music concerts. In summer, many are held outdoors (▷ 37).

A MEMORABLE PLACE TO STAY

De Russie (▷ 112) broke the mold for luxury Rome hotels with its sleek and clean-lined contemporary design.

You want history? The Albergo del Sole al Pantheon (▷ 112) has been a hotel for over 500 years.

The pretty, ivy-covered Raphael (▷ 112) is a tranquil, perfectly situated gem.

ROMANTIC SUPPERS

Dine outdoors in summer; try Panattoni (▷ 74), but almost any restaurant or pizzeria will do.

Vecchia Roma (▷ 60) may not have Rome's best food, but its lovely setting is delightful.

Buy a picnic and take it to the Pincio gardens (▷ 87) to watch the sunset over St. Peter's.

Eat Italian at a traditional trattoria (above) and shop in style on Via Condotti (below)

SPECIALTY SHOPPING

Via dei Coronari (▷ 55–56) and the streets nearby are the places for antiques and sumptuous fabrics.

Stroll down Via Margutta to take in its various art galleries (▷ 10, panel 55).

For designer clothes and accessories, it has to be Via Condotti (▷ 89).

A BREATH OF FRESH AIR

Get away from it all—Villa Borghese and Colle Oppio (below)

The Villa Borghese (▷ 87) park offers numerous walks and shady nooks.
Escape the crowds around the Forum by climbing the Palatine Hill (▷ 34).
If you don't have time to see the Gianicolo and Villa Doria Pamphilj above Trastevere, how about the closer Orto Botanico (▷ 68).

A TASTE OF TRADITION

Long-established Giggetto (▷ 73) and Piperno (▷ 74) serve classic Roman-Jewish cuisine.
As its name suggests, Checchino dal 1887 (▷ 73) has been serving traditional Roman food for over 120 years.
To sample pizza at its best, try Ivo (▷ 74) and Baffetto (▷ 58), who have served pizza to generations of Romans.

A GREAT CUP OF COFFEE

La Tazza d'Oro (▷ 60), a stone's throw from the Pantheon, is a temple to the espresso.
Sant' Eustachio (▷ 60) serves what many locals consider to be Rome's best cup of coffee.
Antico Caffè Brasile (▷ 38) knows its beans— Pope John Paul II once bought his coffee here.

THE WORLD'S BEST CLASSICAL SCULPTURE

After visiting the Musei Capitolini (below) move on to La Tazza d'Ore (above) for a great coffee

Visit the Palazzo Altemps (▷ 42–43) and Palazzo Massimo alle Terme (▷ 82–83), which have manageable and beautifully presented collections.
To see individual sculptural works go to the Museo Capitolini (▷ 28–29), with some of the city's most significant pieces.
The Laocoön (▷ 96) is the most celebrated of the Vatican museums' immense collection of sculptures.

Rome by Area

The Ancient City

The Ancient City is where Rome began, first as a series of settlements on the Palatine Hill, and then as the site of the Foro Romano, the civic, social and political heart of the empire for over 500 years.

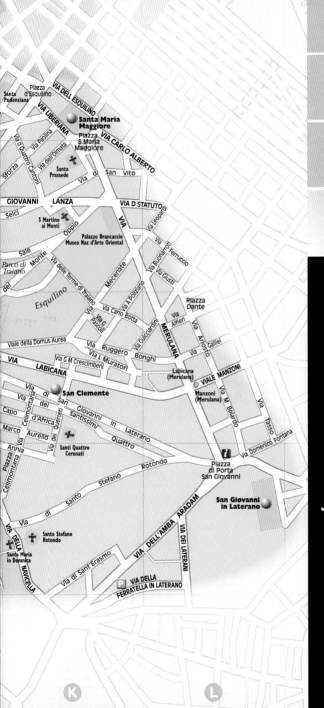

Piazza d'Esquilino
Santa Pudenziana
VIA DELL ESQUILINO
VIA LIBERIANA
Santa Maria Maggiore
Piazza S Maria Maggiore
VIA CARLO ALBERTO
Via di Quattro Cantoni
Via Paolina
Via dell'Olmata
Sforza
Santa Prassede
Via di San Vito
GIOVANNI LANZA
Selci
S Martino ai Monti
Oppio
VIA D STATUTO
VIA
Via Leopardi
Sale
Monte
Palazzo Brancaccio
Museo Naz d'Arte Oriental
Via Buonarroti
Via Ferruccio
Parco di Traiano
del
Via delle terme di Traiano
Mecenate
Via Giusti
Esquilino
Via Carlo Botta
Via A Poliziano
Piazza Dante
Via Alfieri
Viale della Domus Aurea
Via G Pascoli
Via Guicciardini
MERULANA
Via Ariosto
Via Galilei
Via L Muratori
Via Ruggero Bonghi
Via G M Crescimbeni
VIA LABICANA
Labicana (Merulana)
VIALE MANZONI
Via M Boiardo
Via di
San Clemente
Via del San Giovanni in Laterano
Manzoni (Merulana)
Via
Capo
d'Africa
Santissimi
Quattro
Via Tasso
Marco Aurelio
Via dei Querceti
Via Celimontana
Annia
Santi Quattro Coronati
Rotondo
Via Domenico Fontana
Piazza di Porta San Giovanni
Piazza Celimontana
di
Santo Stefano
Via
Santo Stefano Rotondo
San Giovanni in Laterano
VIA DELL'AMBA ARADAM
VIA DEI LATERANI
VIA DELLA NAVICELLA
Santa Maria in Domnica
Via di Sant'Erasmo
VIA DELLA FERRATELLA IN LATERANO
P

K   L

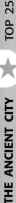
Colosseo

HIGHLIGHTS

● Circumference walls
● Arches: 80 lower arches for the easy admission of crowds
● Doric columns: lowest arcade
● Ionic columns: central arcade
● Corinthian columns: upper arcade
● Underground cells
● Sockets that once housed binding metal clamps
● Vomitoria: interior exits and entrances
● Views from the upper levels

TIP

● The Colosseum's ticket office can be very busy—buy your ticket at the Palatine to avoid waiting, or online.

The Pantheon may be better preserved and the Forum more historically important, but no monument in Rome rivals the majesty of the Colosseum, the largest surviving structure from Roman antiquity.

Awe-inspring The Colosseum was begun by Emperor Vespasian in AD72 and inaugurated by his son, Titus, in AD80 with a gala that saw 5,000 animals slaughtered in a day (and 100 days of continuous games thereafter). Finishing touches to the 55,000-seat stadium were added by Domitian (AD81–96). Three types of columns support the arcades, and the walls are made of brick and volcanic tufa faced with marble blocks, which were once bound together by metal clamps. Its long decline began in the Middle Ages, with the pillaging of stone to build churches and palaces. The

Inside the Colosseum the various tiers are still very evident (far left). The magnificent Colosseum is a daunting sight from all perspectives: close up, from a distance, illuminated at night or under an Italian sunset

desecration ended in 1744, when the structure was consecrated in memory of the Christians supposedly martyred in the arena (later research suggests they weren't). Clearing of the site and excavations began late in the 19th century.

Games Armed combat at the Colosseum went on for some 500 years. Criminals, slaves and gladiators fought each other or wild animals, often to the death. Women and dwarfs also wrestled, and mock sea battles were waged (the arena could be flooded via underground pipes). Spectators exercised the power of life and death over defeated combatants, by waving handkerchiefs to show mercy or by displaying a down-turned thumb to demand the finishing stroke. Survivors' throats were often cut anyway, and the dead were poked with a red-hot iron to make sure they had expired.

THE BASICS

🞣 J7
✉ Piazza del Colosseo, Via dei Fori Imperiali
☎ 06 3996 7700; online booking www.pierreci.it
🕐 May–end Sep daily 9–7.30; Apr and Oct 9–6.30; Nov–end Mar 9–4.30. Last admission 1 hour before closing
🚇 Colosseo
🚌 3, 60, 75, 85, 87, 117, 175 to Piazza del Colosseo
♿ Poor to the interior; limited access from Via Celio Vibenna entrance
💰 Expensive (joint ticket with Palatino)

Foro Romano

TOP
25

The civic and political heart of the Roman Empire was Rome's Forum. Its ruins can be difficult to decipher, but the site is one of the most evocative in the city, the standing stones and fragments conjuring up echoes of a once powerful state.

History The Forum (Foro Romano) started life as a marsh between the Palatine and Capitoline hills, taking its name from a word meaning 'outside the walls'. Later, unfortunately, it became a rubbish dump, and then, having been drained, a marketplace and a religious shrine. In time it acquired all the structures of Rome's burgeoning civic, social and political life. Over the many centuries consuls, emperors and senators have embellished it with magnificent temples, courts and basilicas.

Lone columns and fallen masonary give few clues to the Forum's former impressiveness (far left). Marble Arch of Titus (middle). Detail of relief decoration and frieze on the remains of the Forum market (bottom left). A remaining Corinthian column (bottom right). The view across the Forum, with the Colosseum in the background (right)

Forum and Palatine Two millennia of plunder and decay have left a mish-mash of odd pillars and jumbled stones, which nonetheless can begin to make vivid sense given a plan and some imagination. This strange, empty space is romantic, especially on the Palatine Hill to the south, once covered by a palace.

What to see Today orange trees, oleanders and cypresses line the paths, and grasses and wildflowers flourish among the ancient remains. Worth a visit are the Temple of Antoninus and Faustina, the Colonna di Foca, the Curia, the restored Arch of Septimius Severus, the Portico of the Dei Consentes, the Temple of Saturn, Santa Maria Antiqua (the Forum's oldest church), the aisle of the Basilica of the Emperor Maxentius, the House of the Vestal Virgins and the Arch of Titus.

Musei Capitolini

HIGHLIGHTS

Palazzo Nuovo
● Statue of Marcus Aurelius
● Sculpture: *Capitoline Venus*
● Sculpture: *Dying Gaul*
● Sculpture: *Wounded Amazon*
● Sculpture: *Discobolus*
● Sala degli Imperatori

Palazzo dei Conservatori
● *St. John the Baptist*, Caravaggio
● Bronze: *Lupa Capitolina*
● Bronze: *Spinario*
● Marble figure: *Esquiline Venus*

TIP

● Allow plenty of time and be prepared to concentrate. This is not the easiest museum and not for the fainthearted.

Few in number, but outstanding, the Greek and Roman sculptures in the Capitoline Museums (Palazzo Nuovo and Palazzo dei Conservatori) make a far more accessible introduction to the subject than the Vatican Museums.

Palazzo Nuovo The Capitoline Museums occupy two palaces on opposite sides of the Piazza del Campidoglio and are linked by an underground passage. Both have recently been restored. Designed by Michelangelo, the Palazzo Nuovo (on the north side) contains most of the finest pieces, none greater than the magnificent 2nd-century AD bronze equestrian statue of Marcus Aurelius (just off the main courtyard). Moved here from outside San Giovanni in Laterano in the Middle Ages, it is now restored

Ancient statuary, such as the remains of Constantine's giant statue (far left and middle) and a Satyr (right), make up the collection. Sculpture in the Palazzo dei Conservatori, which holds the largest part of the collection (bottom left). A closer look demonstrates the amazing detail on these works of art (bottom middle and right)

and covered. Among the sculptures inside are celebrated Roman copies in marble of Greek originals, including the *Dying Gaul*, *Wounded Amazon*, *Capitoline Venus* and the discus thrower *Discobolus*. In the Sala degli Imperatori is a portrait gallery of busts of Roman emperors.

Palazzo dei Conservatori This former seat of Rome's medieval magistrates contains an art gallery (the Pinacoteca Capitolina) and a further rich hoard of Classical sculpture. Bronzes include the 1st-century BC *Spinario*, a boy removing a thorn from his foot, and the 5th-century BC Etruscan *Lupa Capitolina*, the famous she-wolf suckling Romulus and Remus (the twins were added by Antonio Pollaiuolo in 1510). Paintings include works by Caravaggio, Velázquez, Titian, Veronese and Van Dyck.

THE BASICS

www.museicapitolini.org

⊞ G6

✉ Musei Capitolini, Piazza del Campidoglio 1

☎ 06 6710 2475 or 06 3996 7800

🕐 Tue–Sun 9–8

🚌 40, 44, 64 and all other services to Piazza Venezia

♿ Poor: steps to Piazza del Campidoglio

💶 Expensive; combined Capitolini Card available

San Clemente

Two of San Clemente's treasures: 12th-century mosaics (left) and the Mithraic temple (right)

THE BASICS

🚇 K7
✉ Via di San Giovanni in Laterano
☎ 06 7045 1018
🕐 Mon–Sat 9–12.30, 3–6, Sun 10–12.30, 3–6
🚌 60, 85, 87, 117, 175 to Piazza del Colosseo or 85, 117, 850 to Via di San Giovanni in Laterano
♿ Church free; excavations moderate

HIGHLIGHTS

● Choir screen
● Chapel of St. Catherine: fresco cycle
● Ciborio: altar canopy
● Apse mosaic: *The Triumph of the Cross*
● Monument to Cardinal Roverella, Giovanni Dalmata (upper church)
● Fresco: *Miracle of San Clemente*
● Fresco: *Legend of Sisinnio*
● Triclinium
● Altar of Mithras: bas-relief of Mithras slaying the bull

No site in Rome reveals as vividly the layers of history that underpin the city as this beautiful medieval ensemble built over a superbly preserved 4th-century church and the remains of a 3rd-century Mithraic temple.

The upper church The present San Clemente, which was named after Rome's fourth pope, was built between 1108 and 1184 to replace an earlier one that was sacked by the Normans in 1084. Almost untouched since, its medieval interior is dominated by the 12th-century marble panels of the choir screen and pulpits and the glittering 12th-century apse mosaic, *The Triumph of the Cross*. Equally captivating are the *Life of St. Catherine* frescos (1428–31) by Masolino da Panicale.

Below ground Steps descend to the lower church, which retains traces of 8th- to 11th-century frescos of San Clemente and the legends of Sts. Alessio and Sisinnio. More steps lead deeper into the twilight world of the best-preserved of the 12 Mithraic temples uncovered in Rome. (Mithraism was a popular, men-only cult, eclipsed by Christianity.) Here are an altar with a bas-relief of Mithras ritually slaying a bull, and the triclinium, used for banquets and rites. Excavations are revealing parts of the temple, and the 1,900-year-old remains of buildings, streets and an underground stream, which you can hear even today, that may have formed part of ancient Rome's drainage system.

Statues on top of the façade seen from afar (left). The beautiful ornate ceiling (right)

San Giovanni in Laterano

San Giovanni's soaring façade can be seen from afar, its distinctive statues rising over the rooftops—a deliberate echo of St. Peter's—reminding us that this is the cathedral church of Rome and the pope's titular see in his role as bishop of Rome.

In the early days A 4th-century palace here provided a meeting place for Pope Miltiades and Constantine (the first Christian emperor), later becoming a focus for Christianity. Earthquakes, fires and Barbarians destroyed the earliest churches on the site, so the façade, modelled on St. Peter's, dates from 1735, and Borromini's interior from 1646. It was the papal residence in Rome until the 14th century, when the popes moved to the Vatican.

Interior treasures Bronze doors from the Forum's Curia usher you into the cavernous interior, its chill whites and greys redeemed by a fabulously ornate ceiling. Other highlights include an apse mosaic by Jacopo Torriti (1288–94) and the beautiful cloister (off the north transept). A high altar reliquary is supposed to contain the heads of St. Peter and St. Paul, and a frescoed tabernacle is attributed to Arnolfo di Cambio and Fiorenzo de Lorenzo.

Step outside Outside are the Scala Santa, reputedly the steps ascended by Christ at his trial in Jerusalem. The octagonal baptistery dates back to the time of Constantine and was the model for many subsequent baptisteries.

THE BASICS

+ L8
✉ Piazza di San Giovanni in Laterano
☎ 06 6988 6433
◷ Church Apr–end Sep daily 7–7 (Oct–end Mar until 6/6.30). Cloisters daily 9–12, 4–6 (until 5 in winter). Scala Santa daily 6.15–12, 3–6.30. Baptistery daily 9–12, 4–7
🚇 San Giovanni
🚌 3, 16, 81, 85, 87, 117, 850 to Piazza di San Giovanni in Laterano
♿ Poor: steps to church
💲 Church, Scala Santa, baptistery free. Cloister inexpensive

HIGHLIGHTS

● Central portal: bronze doors
● Fresco: *Boniface VIII*, attributed to Giotto
● Cappella Corsini
● Frescoed tabernacle
● High altar reliquary
● Apse mosaic, Jacopo Torriti
● Cloister: columns and inlaid marble mosaics
● Papal altar: only the pope can celebrate mass here
● Scala Santa
● Baptistery

Santa Maria Maggiore

TOP 25

Ferdinando Fuga's 18th-century façade (right) conceals a beautiful interior (left)

Santa Maria Maggiore is, justifiably so, considered Rome's finest Early Christian basilica, which is largely thanks to its magnificent mosaic-swathed interior.

History According to a myth, the Virgin appeared to Pope Liberius on 5 August AD352, and told him to build a church exactly where snow would fall the next day. Although it was summer, snow fell, marking the outlines of a basilica on the Esquiline Hill. Legend aside, the church probably dates from AD430, though the campanile (the tallest in Rome at 75m/246ft) was added in 1377 and the interior and exterior were altered in the 13th and 18th centuries. The coffered ceiling, attributed to Giuliano da Sangallo, was reputedly gilded with the first gold to arrive from the New World, a gift from Spain to Alexander VI (note his Borgia bull emblems).

Rich decoration Beyond the general grandeur, the main treasures are the 36 mosaics in the architraves of the nave, 5th-century depictions of the lives of Moses, Abraham, Isaac and Jacob, framed by some 40 ancient columns. Also compelling are the mosaics in the loggia and on the triumphal arch. In the 13th-century apse are mosaics by Jacopo Torriti, the pinnacle of Rome's medieval mosaic tradition. Other highlights include the Cappella Sistina (tomb of Pope Sixtus V) by Domenico Fontana, 1588; the Cappella Paolina, built by Paul V (1611); and Giovanni di Cosma's tomb of Cardinal Rodriguez (1299). The high altar reputedly contains a relic of Christ's crib.

More to See

ARCO DI COSTANTINO

Triumphal arches, like celebratory columns, were usually raised as monuments to military achievement, in this case the victory of Emperor Constantine over his imperial rival Maxentius. It was one of the last great monuments to be built in ancient Rome, and at 21m (69ft) high and 26m (85ft) wide it is also the largest and best-preserved of the city's arches. Most of its reliefs were taken from earlier buildings, partly out of pragmatism and partly out of a desire to link Constantine's glories with those of the past. The battle scenes of the central arch show Trajan at war with the Dacians, while another describes a boar hunt and sacrifice to Apollo.

➕ J7 ✉ Piazza del Colosseo-Via di San Gregorio, Via dei Fori Imperiali 🕐 Always open 🚇 Colosseo 🚌 60, 75, 85, 87, 117, 175, C3 to Piazza del Colosseo 💷 Free

CIRCO MASSIMO

This enormous grassy arena follows the outline of a stadium once capable of seating 300,000 people. Created to satisfy the passionate Roman appetite for chariot racing, and the prototype for almost all subsequent racecourses, it was begun around 326BC and modified frequently before the occasion of its last recorded use under Totila the Ostrogoth in AD549. Much of the original structure was robbed of its stone—old monuments were often ransacked for building materials—but the *spina* (the circuit's dividing wall) remains, marked by a row of cypresses, the ruins of the imperial box and the open arena, now a public park. Avoid after dark.

➕ H8 ✉ Via del Circo Massimo 🕐 Always open 🚇 Circo Massimo 🚌 60, 75, 81, 175, 628, 673, C3 to Piazza di Porta Capena 💷 Free

FORI IMPERIALI

The five colonnaded areas just down the road from the Colesseum were once the Imperial Fora, built as commerical and political meeting places by successive emperors. Plundered remorselessly over the centuries, today's ruins seem at first glance little more

Cast in evening light, the Arch of Constantine

Imperial Forum with the Trajans Market in the foreground

than a jumble of columns and tumbled stone, so take time to get your bearings. Excavations are still ongoing, and over 15,000sq m (160,000sq ft) have been unearthed, representing more than half the original fora—and there's still more to discover.

🚼 H6 ⊠ Via dei Fori Imperiali ☎ 06 679 7786; Visitor Centre 06 679 7702 🅾 Guided tour only, check with Visitor Centre for times 🚇 Colosseo 🚌 75, 84, 87, 117, 175 to Via dei Fori Imperiali 🚽 Moderate

MERCATI TRAIANEI

Trajan's markets were a group of commercial buildings constructed at the beginning of the 2nd century AD as a semicircular range of halls on three levels. Two survive in excellent condition, together with many of the 150 booths that once traded rare and expensive commodities.

🚼 H6 ⊠ Via IV Novembre 94 ☎ 06 679 0048; reservations 06 6978 0532 🅾 Apr–end Sep, Tue–Sun 9–6.30; Oct–end Mar, Tue–Sun 9–4.30 🚇 Cavour 🚌 H, 40, 60, 64, 70, 117, 170 and other routes to Via IV Novembre 🚽 Expensive

PALATINO E ORTI FARNESIANI

After a stroll around the Forum it's worth making time to climb the Palatine Hill to enjoy this peaceful spot. Orange groves, cypresses and endless drowsy corners, all speckled with flowers and ancient stones, make up the Orti Farnesiani, which were laid out in the 16th century over the ruins of the palace that once stood here.

🚼 H7 ⊠ Entrances from Via di San Gregorio 30 and other entrances to the Roman Forum ☎ 06 3996 7700 🅾 Daily 9–1 hour before dusk 🚇 Colosseo 🚌 75, 84, 87, 117, 175 to Via dei Fori Imperiali 🚽 Expensive (joint ticket with Colosseum)

PIAZZA DEL CAMPIDOGLIO

This piazza was designed by Michelangelo for Emperor Charles V's triumphal entry into Rome in 1536 on the Capitoline, the most famous of Rome's seven hills and the hub of the Roman Empire. The magnificent buildings that stand on three sides of the square—the Palazzo Senatorio, the Palazzo Nuovo and the Palazzo dei Conservatori, were part of his scheme.

Mercati Trainei terraced up the Quirinal Hill   *Remains laid out beneath the ruins on Palatine Hill*

G6 ✉ Piazza del Campidoglio
Ⓜ Colosseo 🚌 All services to Piazza Venezia

SAN PIETRO IN VINCOLI

Hidden in a narrow back street, San Pietro in Vincoli is a thoroughly appealing church. Drop by to admire Michelangelo's statue of Moses, one of the most powerful of all the artist's monumental sculptures. San Pietro in Vincoli takes its name from the chains (*vincoli*) proudly kept in the coffer with bronze doors under the high altar. According to tradition they are the chains used to bind St. Peter while he was held captive in the Mamertine prison. The 20 columns of its interior arcade came from a Roman temple.

✚ J6 ✉ Piazza di San Pietro in Vincoli 4a ☎ 06 488 2865 🕐 Daily 8–12/12.30, 3/3.30–6/7 Ⓜ Colosseo or Cavour 🚌 75, 84 to Via Cavour or 60, 75, 85, 87, 117, 175 to Piazza del Colosseo 🚻 Good 🎟 Free

SANTA MARIA IN ARACOELI

Perched atop the Capitoline Hill, Santa Maria in Aracoeli, with its glorious ceiling, fine frescos and soft chandelier-lit interior, is a calm retreat from the ferocious traffic of Piazza Venezia. The flight of 124 steep steps approaching Santa Maria was built in 1348 to celebrate either the end of a plague epidemic or the Holy Year proclaimed for 1350. The church is first recorded in AD574, but even then it was old. Most of the present structure dates from 1260.

✚ G/H6 ✉ Piazza d'Aracoeli ☎ 06 679 8155 🕐 Daily 7–12, 4–6 or dusk 🚌 40, 44, 46, 62, 64, 70, 80 and all other services to Piazza Venezia 🚻 Poor: steep steps to main entrance or steps to Piazza del Campidoglio 🎟 Free

VILLA CELIMONTANA

Set on one of the southern hills of ancient Rome and scattered with the remains of ancient buildings, this is one of Rome's lesser-known parks, easily accessible from the Colosseum and San Giovanni in Laterano.

✚ J8 ✉ Piazza della Navicella 🕐 Daily 7–dusk 🚌 3 to Via dei Parco del Celio or 117, 673 to Via Claudia 🎟 Free

A statue of Marcus Aurelius takes centre stage in Piazza del Campidoglio

Michelangelo's monumental statue of Moses, in the church of San Pietro in Vincoli

Shopping

BOTTEGA DEL CIOCCOLATO

A blissful Italian chocolate shop. Most goodies are produced from a 19th-century Piedmont recipe; others are 'secrets of old masters'. Period cupboards and shelves, and a large mirror reflecting the chocolate creations along the wall in jars.

✚ J6 ✉ Via Leonina 82
☎ 06 482 1473 ◷ Mon–Sat 9.30–7.30

COIN

www.coin.it
One of Rome's most popular department stores is a modern, mainly glass building with cosmetics, home furnishings, kitchenware, toys and fashions. The top floor is dedicated to home exhibitions. Prices are higher than in the average store.

✚ M8 ✉ Piazza Appio 7
☎ 06 709 0020 ◷ Daily 9.30–8

MERCATO DI VIA SANNIO

This market in the shadow of San Giovanni in Laterano sells bags, belts, shoes, toys and inexpensive clothes. Other stands nearby peddle more interesting bric-a-brac.

✚ M8 ✉ Via Sannio
◷ Mon–Fri 10–1.30, Sat 10–6

PANELLA

For over a century, Panella has sold dozens of varieties of bread and cakes, and it has the largest selection of homemade *grissini* (bread stick) in Rome. The back rooms are packed with hard-to-find ingredients.

✚ K6 ✉ Via Merulana 54–55
☎ 06 487 2344 ◷ Mon–Sat 8–2, 5–8, Sun 8–2

Entertainment and Nightlife

CAVOUR 313

At the Forum end of Via Cavour, this easily missed wine bar has a relaxed, student feel. Good snacks from the bar and wine by the glass or bottle.

✚ H6 ✉ Via Cavour 313
☎ 06 678 5496
◷ Mon–Sat 12.30–2.30, 7.30–12.30 (also Sun 7.30–12.30 Oct–end May)
🚌 75, 84, 117 to Via Cavour or 84, 85, 87, 175 to Via dei Fori Imperiali

DRUID'S DEN

Friendly and realistic Irish pub that appeals to Romans and expats alike. Also try The Fiddler's Elbow, a popular sister pub around the corner at Via dell'Olmata 43.

✚ K6 ✉ Via San Martino ai Monti 28 ☎ 06 4890 4781

MUSIC OUTDOORS

Alfresco recitals often take place throughout the city in summer. Locations include the cloisters of Santa Maria della Pace; the Villa Doria Pamphilj; in the grounds of the Villa Giulia; and in the Area Archeologica del Teatro di Marcello from July to September (as part of the Estate al Tempietto, also known as the Concerti del Tempietto). Note that the venues may change from year to year.

◷ Mon–Fri 5pm–12.30am, Sat–Sun 4pm–1am
🚌 Cavour 🚌 75, 84, 117 to Via Cavour or 16, 70, 71, 360 to Piazza Santa Maria Maggiore

TEATRO COLOSSEO

www.teatrocolosseo.it
In the shadow of the mighty Colosseum, this venue is a rarity for Rome—a theatre that sometimes stages English-language plays. It showcases young directors and actors, and the small stage suits one-man shows.

✚ J7 ✉ Via Capo d'Africa 5
☎ 06 700 4932 ◷ Sep–end Jun Mon–Sat 10–1, 3–7
🚌 Colosseo 🚌 30

Restaurants

PRICES

Prices are approximate, based on a 3-course meal for one person.

€€€	over €50
€€	€30–€50
€	under €30

AGATA E ROMEO (€€€)

www.agataeromei.it

It is worth putting up with a less-than-perfect position south of Termini because this cosy, family-run restaurant serves some of the city's best and most imaginative modern Roman cooking.

K6 Via Carlo Alberto 45 06 446 6115 Mon–Fri 12.30–2.30, 7.30–10; closed 2 weeks in Jan and Aug 70, 71, 360 to Via Carlo Alberto

ANTICO CAFFÈ BRASILE (€)

Superb variety of beans and ground coffee sold from huge sacks or at the bar. Try the 'Pope's blend': John Paul II bought his coffee here before his pontificate.

J6 Via dei Serpenti 23 06 488 2319 Mon– Sat 6am–8pm, Sun 7–7 60, 63, 64, 70, 117, 170 to Via Nazionale or 75, 84, 117 to Via Cavour

CHARLY'S SAUCIÈRE (€€)

Homey and established, offering reliable French and Swiss staples.

L8 Via di San Giovanni in Laterano 268–270 06 7049 5666 Tue–Fri 12.30–2.30, Mon–Sat 7.30–10.30; closed 2 weeks in Aug 85, 117, 850 to Via San Giovanni in Laterano

GRAN CAFFÉ MARTINI E ROSSI (€)

Bar/restaurant popular with locals, and what better location could it have than looking across to the Palatine Hill, with the Colosseo across the road? Good-value all-inclusive menus, plus snacks and vegetarian dishes.

J7 Piazza del Colosseo 06 700 4431 Daily 9am–1am 85, 87, 117

HASEKURA (€–€€)

Rome's best Japanese food; good set-price menus, with the Forum and Colosseum close by.

J6 Via dei Serpenti 27 06 483 648 Mon–Sat noon–2.30, 7–10.30; closed Aug Cavour 71, 84 to Via Cavour

ROMAN SPECIALTIES

Roman favourites—though they are by no means confined to the city—include pastas like *bucatini all'amatriciana* (tomato sauce, salt pork and chilli peppers); *spaghetti alla carbonara* (egg, bacon, pepper and cheese); and *gnocchi alla Romana* (small potato or semolina dumplings with tomato or butter). The best-known main course is *saltimbocca alla Romana* (veal scallops with ham and sage, cooked in wine and butter). Also traditional are *trippa* (tripe), *cervelli* (brains) and *coda alla vaccinara* (oxtail).

NERONE (€€)

A small, friendly, old-fashioned *trattoria* just a few steps north of the Colosseum that is best known for its antipasti buffet and simple Abruzzese cooking. Has a handful of outside tables.

J7 Via delle Terme di Tito 96 06 481 7952 Mon–Sat 12–3, 7–11; closed Aug Colosseo 60, 75, 85, 87, 117, 175, 810, 850 to Piazza del Colosseo

PASQUILINO (€€)

A simple, long-established *trattoria* with good, robust food a few minutes east of the Colosseum.

K7 Via dei Santissimi Quattro 66 06 700 4576 Tue–Sun 12.30–2.30, 7.30–11; closed 2 weeks in Aug Colosseo 85 to Via di San Giovanni in Laterano

SAN CLEMENTE (€)

This bar/pizzeria is a great place to refuel between the Colosseo and the basilica of San Giovanni in Laterano. Three vaulted rooms and a terrace offer decent inexpensive food.

K7 Via di San Giovanni Laterano 124 06 7045 0944 Daily 7am–1am Colosseo or San Giovanni 85, 87, 117 to Via di San Giovanni in Laterano

Central Rome

Here, most of the great churches, palaces and squares of the city's medieval, baroque and Renaissance heyday sit beside museums, monuments and cobbled streets filled with cafés, shops and restaurants.

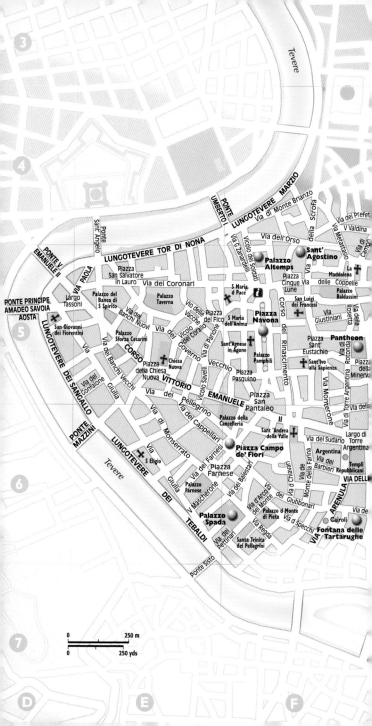

3

Tevere

4

PONTE UMBERTO I

LUNGOTEVERE MARZIO

Via di Monte Brianzo

Via della Scrofa

Via dei Prefet

V Valdina

Via di Campo

Via dell'Orso

Via delle Coppelle

Via del Metastasio

Ponte Sant'Angelo

LUNGOTEVERE TOR DI NONA

Vicolo del Curato

Via G Zanardelli

Vicolo dei Soldati

Sant' Agostino

La Maddalena

PONTE V EMANUELE II

VIA PAOLA

Piazza San Salvatore in Lauro

Via dei Coronari

S Maria d Pace

Palazzo Altemps

Piazza Cinque Vie Lune

Palazzo Baldassini

Largo Tassoni

Palazzo del Banco di S Spirito

Via del Banchi Nuovi

Palazzo Taverna

Vicolo delle Vacche

Piazza del Fico

S Maria dell'Anima

Piazza Navona

Corso del Rinascimento

San Luigi dei Francesi

Via Giustiniani

Via della Rosetta

PONTE PRINCIPE AMADEO SAVOIA AOSTA

San Giovanni dei Fiorentini

LUNGOTEVERE DEI SANGALLO

Via del Confalone

Via dei Banchi Vecchi

CORSO

Palazzo Sforza Cesarini

Vicolo del Corallo

Via del Governo Vecchio

Via di Parione

Sant'Agnese in Agone

Palazzo Pamphili

Piazza Sant' Eustachio

Sant'Ivo alla Sapienza

Pantheon

Piazza della Rotonda

Piazza della Minerva

5

Giulia

Piazza della Chiesa Nuova

Chiesa Nuova

VITTORIO

Via dei Pellegrini

Vicolo Savelli

EMANUELE

Piazza Pasquino

Piazza San Pantaleo

Via di Torre Argentina

Via Monterone

Via della

Ponte Mazzini

Via di Monserrato

Via dei Cappellari

Palazzo della Cancelleria

Sant' Andrea della Valle

II

Largo di Torre Argentina

Templi Repubblicani

6

Tevere

LUNGOTEVERE DEI TEBALDI

Via di Balestrari

Piazza Campo de' Fiori

Via dei Chiavari

Via del Sudario

Via dei Barbieri

Argentina

VIA DELL

Giulia

S Eligio

Piazza Farnese

Via dei Farnesi

Via d'Arco del Monte

Via di Giubbonari

ARENULA

Via de

V Mascherone

Palazzo Farnese

Palazzo Spada

Via del Pettinari

Via dei Giubbonari

Palazzo d Monte di Pieta

Via d'Specchi

Via Arenula

VIA

Cairoli

Fontana delle Tartarughe

Santa Trinita dei Pellegrini

Via Reggia

Ponte Sisto

7

0   250 m

0   250 yds

D   E   F

Via in Lucina

Via dell'Impresa

Palazzo di Montecitorio

Palazzo Chigi

Colonna di Marco Aurelio

Piazza Colonna

Via del Corso

Via delle Muratte

Museo Nazionale delle Paste Alimentari

VIA DEL QUIRINALE

Palazzo del Quirinale

Piazza di Pietra

Via d'Aquiro

Via del Seminario

Sant'Ignazio di Loyola

Via dell'Umiltà

Piazza del Quirinale

Palazzo Consulta

Via Piacenza

Via di Parma

Vlo Mazzarino

VIA XXIV MAGGIO

Santa Maria sopra Minerva

Palazzo Sciarra

Palazzo Odescalchi

Sant'Apostoli

Palazzo-Galleria Doria Pamphilj

Via del Marmo

Via del Gesù

Palazzo Altieri

Piazza del Santi Apostoli

Via del Corso

Palazzo Colonna

Via del Marcello

Villa Colonna

Via della Pilotta

VIA IV NOVEMBRE

Museo del Palazzo Venezia

Piazza Venezia

Via di S.Eufemia

pigna

VIA DEL PLEBISCITO

San Marco

Ch del Gesù

VIA DI SAN MARCO

BOTTEGHE OSCURE

Crypta Balbi

Via del Delfini

d'Aracoeli

Via Falegnami

Santa Maria in Campitelli

G

H

Central Rome

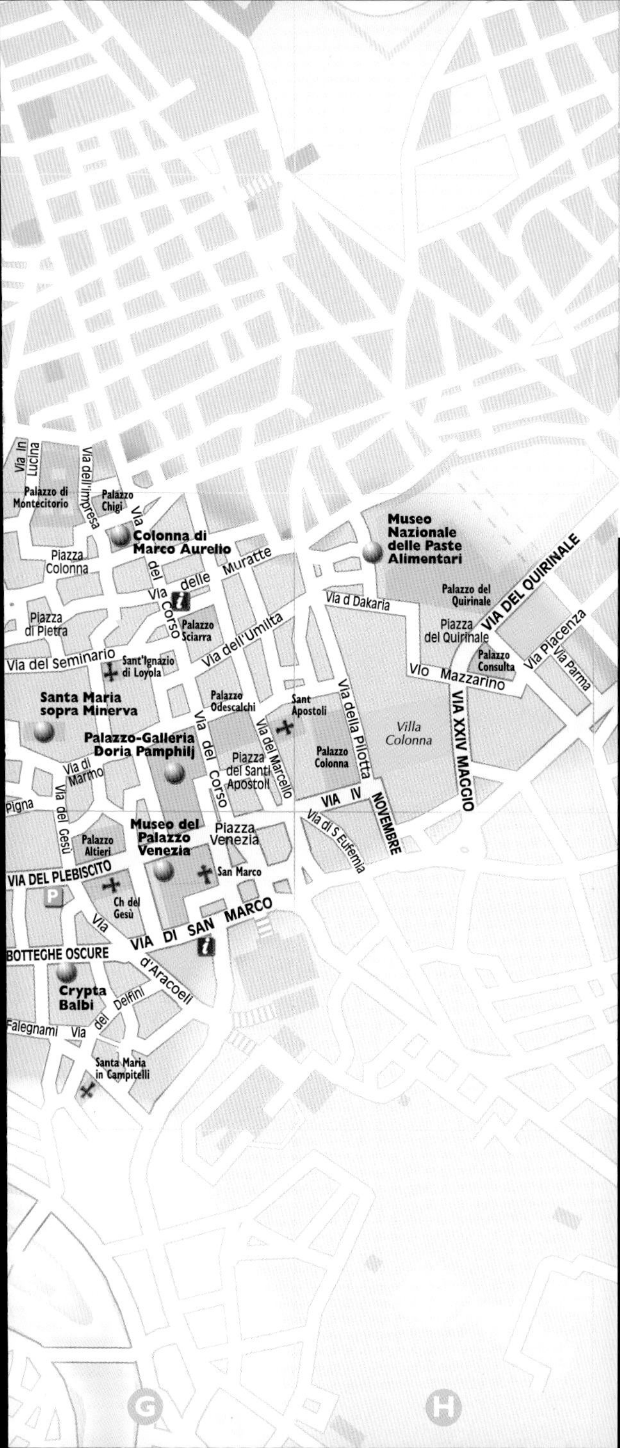

Palazzo Altemps

- Aphrodite's Throne
- Galatian Soldier statue
- Courtyard loggia
- Satyr pouring wine
- Head of Aphrodite

TIPS

- A combined ticket is available, which includes entry to the Palazzo Altemps, Palazzo Massimo alle Terme and other sights.

- Tickets can be prebooked at www.pierreci.it or call ☎ 06 3996 7700 (Mon–Sat).

This beautiful building epitomizes the best of Renaissance urban architecture, while its series of elegant rooms provides the perfect setting for some of the finest of Rome's Classical sculpture.

The building   Rome's Museo Nazionale Romano (National Roman Museum) is housed in two superbly restored buildings; the Palazzo Massimo alle Terme (▷ 82–83) near the station and here in the Palazzo Altemps, whose odd-sounding name is the Italian corruption of the German name von Hohenemps. Mainly constructed in the 15th century, the building houses a series of charming and intimate rooms, many with vaulted ceilings. One gives access to a splendidly frescoed loggia overlooking the comings and goings of a harmonious inner courtyard. The best time to get

A colossal exhibit, just one example from this top-class collection of Classical sculpture (left). Statues watch over the Palazzo Altemps' peaceful courtyard (middle). Statuary exhibited in the arcades (bottom middle). The Painted Loggia on the upper floor (right)

a sense of the building's history is as dusk falls, when the rooms and exhibits are imaginatively lit.

The collections The *palazzo* is home to the famous Ludovisi Collection, amassed by Cardinal Ludovico Ludovisi in the 17th century, as well as the Altemps collection, Egyptian antiques and portraits. Downstairs look for the *Tiber Apollo*, so called because it was found in the bed of the river in the late 19th century, and the two gigantic statues of Athena. Upstairs, the star of the collection the Ludovisi Throne, is probably a Greek sculpture dedicated as a throne for Aphrodite, the protectress of sailors. From the 5th century BC, the delicate carving portrays the goddess rising from the sea foam, her draperies clinging to her. Do not miss the statue of the *Galatian Soldier and His Wife Committing Suicide*, apparently commissioned by Julius Caesar.

THE BASICS

⊞ F5
✉ Piazza Sant' Apollinare 44
☎ 06 683 3759 or 06 3996 7700
⏰ Tue–Sun 9–7.45
🚌 30, 70, 87, 116, 492, 628 to Corso del Rinascimento
♿ Moderate

Palazzo-Galleria Doria Pamphilj

TOP 25

HIGHLIGHTS

● *Religion Succoured by Spain* (labelled 10) and *Salome* (29), Titian
● *Portrait of Two Venetians* (23), Raphael
● *Maddalena* (40) and *Rest on the Flight into Egypt* (42), Caravaggio
● *Birth and Marriage of the Virgin* (174/176), Giovanni di Paolo
● *Nativity* (200), Parmigianino
● *Innocent X*, Velázquez
● *Innocent X*, Bernini
● *Battle of the Bay of Naples* (317), Pieter Brueghel the Elder
● Salone Verde
● Saletta Gialla

TIPS

● Use the audioguide, which is included in the price and helps make sense of what you're seeing.
● The paintings are not well lit so it is better to visit during the daylight hours.

One of Rome's largest palaces that contains one of the city's finest patrician art collections and offers the chance to admire some of the sumptuously decorated rooms of its private apartments.

A dynasty Little in the bland exterior of the Palazzo Doria Pamphilj prepares you for the glory of the beautiful rooms that lie within. The core of the building, which was built over the foundations of a storehouse dating back to ancient times, was erected in 1435, and it has withstood countless alterations and owners. The Doria Pamphilj dynasty was formed by yoking together the Doria, a famous Genoese seafaring clan, and the Pamphilj, a Rome-based patrician family. Most people come here for the paintings, but—when open—you can enjoy a guided tour around some

This magnificent palace is at the middle of lovely parkland laid out by Prince Camillo Pamphilj in the mid-17th century (left). Inside the galleries are lavishly decorated with painted ceilings and the walls adorned with golden framed mirrors (right)

of the private apartments in the 1,000-room palace. The most impressive is the Saletta Gialla (Yellow Room), decorated with 12 Gobelin tapestries made for Louis XV. In the Salone Verde (Green Room) are three important paintings: *Annunciation* by Filippo Lippi, *Portrait of a Gentleman* by Lorenzo Lotto and *Andrea Doria* (a famous admiral) by Sebastiano del Piombo.

Labyrinth of masterpieces The Pamphilj's art collection is displayed in ranks in four broad galleries. As the works are numbered, not labelled, it's worth investing in a guidebook from the ticket office. The finest painting is the famous Velázquez portrait, *Innocent X* (1650), a likeness that captured the pope's weak and suspicious nature so adroitly that Innocent is said to have lamented that it was 'too true, too true'.

THE BASICS

www.doriapamphilj.it
⊞ G5
✉ Piazza del Collegio Romano 1a
☎ 06 679 7323
🕐 Fri–Wed 10–5. Apartments currently closed for restoration
🚇 Barberini
🚌 60, 62, 85, 95, 160, 492 and all other services to Piazza Venezia
♿ Good
💶 Gallery expensive. Apartments moderate

Pantheon

HIGHLIGHTS

- Façade inscription
- The pedimented portico
- Original Roman doors
- Marble interior and pavement
- Coffered dome and oculus
- Tomb of Raphael
- Royal tombs

TIP

● The Pantheon is often very crowded. To make the most of your visit, go on a weekday or early in the morning.

No other monument suggests the grandeur of ancient Rome as magnificently as this temple whose early conversion to a place of Christian worship has rendered it the most perfect of the city's ancient monuments.

Temple and church The greatest surviving complete Roman structure, built by Emperor Hadrian from AD118–28, the Pantheon replaced a temple of 27BC by Marcus Agrippa, son-in-law of Augustus. (Modestly, Hadrian retained the original inscription proclaiming it as Agrippa's work.) It became the church of Santa Maria ad Martyres in AD609 (the bones of martyrs were brought here from the Catacombs) and is now a shrine to Italy's 'immortals', including the artist Raphael and kings Vittore Emanuele II and Umberto I.

The sun pours through the opening in the Pantheon's roof (far left and bottom middle). Raphael's Tomb (middle). Giacomo della Porta's fountain in Piazza della Rotonda (bottom). Sixteen massive Egyptian granite columns support the portico (bottom left and right)

An engineering marvel Massive and simple from the outside, the Pantheon is at its most breathtaking inside, where the scale, harmony and symmetry of the dome in particular are more apparent. The world's largest dome until 1882 (when it was surpassed in the English spa resort of Buxton), it has a diameter of 43.3m (142ft)—equal to its height from the floor. Weight and stresses were reduced by rows of coffers in the ceiling, and the use of progressively lighter materials from the base to the crown. The central oculus, 9m (30ft) in diameter and clearly intended to inspire meditation on the heavens above, lets light (and rain) fall onto the marble pavement far below. Take time to relax in one of Piazza della Rotanda's many cafés to enjoy and admire the exterior view of the Pantheon and the atmosphere of the lively piazza.

THE BASICS

➕ F5
✉ Piazza della Rotonda
☎ 06 6830 0230
🕐 Mon–Sat 8.30–7.30, Sun 9–6, public holidays 9–1
🚇 Spagna
🚌 116, 119 to Piazza della Rotonda or 40, 64, 70 and all other services to Largo di Torre Argentina
♿ Good
🖐 Free

Piazza Campo de' Fiori

TOP
25

Vibrant market stalls surround the statue of Giordano Bruno in Campo dei Fiori

THE BASICS

🚇 F6

✉ Piazza Campo de' Fiori

🕐 Market Mon–Sat 7–1.30

🚌 40, 46, 62, 64 to Corso Vittorio Emanuele II or H, 8, 46, 62, 64, 70, 87 to Largo di Torre Argentina

♿ Cobbled streets and some curbs around piazza

💷 Free

HIGHLIGHTS

● Street market
● Wine bar Vineria Reggio
● Statue of Giordano Bruno
● Palazzo Farnese, Piazza Farnese
● Palazzo della Cancelleria, Piazza della Cancelleria
● Palazzo Pio Righetti
● Via Giulia
● Santa Maria dell'Orazione e Morte: church door decorated in stone skulls
● Via dei Baullari

There is nowhere more relaxing in Rome to sit and watch the world go by than Campo de' Fiori, a lovely old piazza whose fruit, vegetable and fish market makes it one of the liveliest and most vivid corners of the old city.

Ancient square Campo de' Fiori, or the 'Field of Flowers', was turned in the Middle Ages from a meadow facing the ancient Theatre of Pompey (55BC; now Palazzo Pio Righetti) into one of the city's most exclusive residential and business districts. By the 15th century it was surrounded by busy inns and bordellos, some run by the infamous courtesan Vannozza Catanei, mistress of the Borgia pope Alexander VI. By 1600 it had also become a place of execution; Giordano Bruno was burned for heresy on the spot marked by his cowled statue.

Present day Just sit back and soak up the atmosphere. Students, foreigners, locals and tramps mingle with the market vendors shouting their wares, while the cafés, bars and the wonderfully dingy wine bar at No. 15 will have you relishing the street life. One block south lies Piazza Farnese, dominated by the Palazzo Farnese, a Renaissance masterpiece partly designed by Michelangelo and begun in 1516. It is now home to the French Embassy. One block west is the Palazzo della Cancelleria (1485), once the papal chancellery. The nearby Via Giulia, Via dei Baullari, the busy Via dei Cappellari and Via del Pellegrino are all wonderful streets to explore.

Bernini's fountain and obelisk lie at the heart of Piazza Navona

Piazza Navona

Piazza di Spagna may be more elegant and Campo de' Fiori more vivid, but Piazza Navona, with its atmospheric echoes of a 2,000-year history, is a glorious place to amble or stop for a drink at a sun-drenched table.

Shaping history Piazza Navona owes its unmistakable elliptical shape to a stadium and racetrack built here in AD86 by Emperor Domitian. From the Circus Agonalis—the stadium for athletic games—comes the piazza's present name, rendered in medieval Latin as *in agone*, and then in Rome's strangulated dialect as *'n 'agona*. The stadium was used until well into the Middle Ages for festivals and competitions. The square owes its present appearance to its rebuilding by Pope Innocent X in 1644.

Around the piazza Bernini's spirited Fontana dei Quattro Fiumi (1651), the 'Fountain of the Four Rivers', dominates. Unveiled in 1651, it has four figures that represent the four rivers of Paradise (the Nile, Ganges, Danube and Plate), and the four 'corners' of the world (Africa, Asia, Europe and America). On the west side is the baroque Sant' Agnese (1652–57), its façade designed by Borromini. Beside it stands the Palazzo Pamphilj, commissioned by Innocent X and now the Brazilian Embassy. Further afield, San Luigi dei Francesi is famous for three superlative Caravaggio paintings, and Santa Maria della Pace for a cloister by Bramante and Raphael's frescos of the four *Sybils*.

THE BASICS

🔛 F5
✉ Piazza Navona
🚇 Spagna
🚌 30, 70, 51, 87, 116, 492, 628 to Corso del Rinascimento or 40, 46, 62, 64 to Corso Vittorio Emanuele II

HIGHLIGHTS

● Fontana dei Quattro Fiumi
● Fontana del Moro (south)
● Fontana del Nettuno (north)
● Palazzo Pamphilj
● San Luigi dei Francesi (Via Santa Giovanna d' Arco)
● Santa Maria dell'Anima (Via della Pace)

Santa Maria sopra Minerva

Soaring Gothic arches (left). Bernini's elephant (middle).Tomb of St. Catherine (right)

THE BASICS

✚ G5

✉ Piazza della Minerva 42

☎ 06 679 3926

🕐 Mon–Sat 7–7, Sun 8–7 (10–6 in winter)

Ⓢ Spagna

🚌 H, 8, 30, 40, 46, 62, 64, 70, 81, 87 to Lago di Torre Argentina or 119 to Piazza della Rotonda

♿ Stepped access to church

💲 Free

HIGHLIGHTS

● Porch to the Cappella Carafa

● Frescos: *St. Thomas Aquinas* and *The Assumption*, Filippino Lippi, in the Cappella Carafa

● *Risen Christ*, Michelangelo

● Relics of St. Catherine of Siena, and preserved room in sacristy where she died

● Tombs of Clement VII and Leo X, Antonio da Sangallo

● Tomb slab of Fra Angelico

● Tomb of Giovanni Alberini, Mino da Fiesole or Agostino di Duccio

● Monument to Maria Raggi

● Tomb of Francesco Tornabuoni, Mino da Fiesole

Remarkable in having retained many Gothic features despite Rome's love for the baroque, behind its plain façade Santa Maria sopra Minerva is a cornucopia of tombs, paintings and Renaissance sculpture.

Florentine influences Originally founded in the 8th century over ruins of a temple to Minerva, the church was built in 1280 to a design by two Florentine Dominican monks who modelled it on their own church, Santa Maria Novella. Before entering the church, notice its strange but charming statue of an elephant supporting an ancient Greek obelisk in the piazza outside. It was designed by Bernini in the 17th century.

Inside The interior of the church abounds with beautiful works such as the Cappella Carafa (whose fine porch is attributed to Giuliano da Maiano), and Michelangelo's calm statue *The Risen Christ* (1521), left of the high altar. Filippino Lippi painted the celebrated frescos *St. Thomas Aquinas* and the *Assumption* (1488–93). Among other sculptures are the tombs of Francesco Tornabuoni (1480) and that of Giovanni Alberini, the latter decorated with reliefs of Hercules (15th century). Both are attributed to Mino da Fiesole. Other works include Fra Angelico's tomb slab (1455); the tombs of Medici popes Clement VII and Leo X (1536) by Antonio da Sangallo the Younger; and Bernini's monument to Maria Raggi (1643). St. Catherine of Siena, one of Italy's patron saints, is buried beneath the high altar.

More to See

COLONNA DI MARCO AURELIO

The Column of Marcus Aurelius (AD 180–96) was built to celebrate Aurelius's military triumphs over hostile north European tribes. It is composed of 27 separate drums of Carrara marble welded into a seamless whole, and is done with a continuous spiral of bas-reliefs commemorating episodes from the victorious campaigns. Aurelius is depicted no fewer than 59 times, though curiously never actually in battle. The summit statue is of St. Paul, crafted by Domenico Fontana in 1589 to replace the 60th depiction of Aurelius.

🗺 G5 ✉ Piazza Colonna, Via del Corso 🕐 Always open 🚇 Barberini 🚌 62, 63, 85, 95, 117, 119 and all routes to to Via del Corso 💲 Free

CRYPTA BALBI

This museum, part of the Museo Nazionale Romano, contains part of a theatre built in 13BC, along with a rich collection of objects to illustrate social, economic and urban planning changes from ancient times, through the Middle Ages up to the present day. Two other sections have displays of vases, glassware, mosaics and other items dating from between the 5th and 8th centuries.

🗺 G6 ✉ Via delle Botteghe Oscure 31 🕐 06 3996 7700 🕐 Tue–Sun 9–7.45 🚇 Barberini 🚌 30,40, 46, 62, 64, 70, 492, 628, 780, 787, 916 to Largo di Torre Argentina ✋ Expensive

FONTANA DELLE TARTARUGHE

This tiny fountain (1581–84) is one of Rome's most delightful sights, thanks to the tortoises, probably added by Bernini in 1658 (the current bronze sculptures are copies).

🗺 F6 ✉ Piazza Mattei 🚌 H, 8, 63, 630, 780 to Via Arenula or 30, 70, 87, 116 and other services to Largo di Torre Argentina

MUSEO NAZIONALE DELLE PASTE ALIMENTARI

www.pastainmuseum.it

An unusual museum dedicated to Italy's best-loved and best-known food—pasta. It traces the history and evolution of pasta and of the

Colonna di Marco Aurelio

Detail of the Fontana delle Tartarughe showing a boy reaching up to a tortoise

manufacturing processes, from early grindstones for milling the wheat to modern industrial pasta machinery.
✠ H5 ✉ Piazza Scanderberg 117 🕒 06 699 1119 🕒 Daily 9.30–5.30 🚇 Barberini 🚌 52, 53, 61, 62, 63, 71, 80, 85, 160, 850 to Piazza San Silvestro 🖐 Expensive

MUSEO DEL PALAZZO VENEZIA
Built in 1455 for Pietro Barbo (later Pope Paul II), and one of the first Renaissance palaces, the former Venetian Embassy became the property of the state in 1916; Mussolini harangued the crowds from the balconies. The museum hosts travelling exhibitions and a fine permanent collection that includes Renaissance paintings, sculpture, armour, ceramics, silverware and objets d'art.
✠ G6 ✉ Palazzo Venezia, Via del Plebiscito 118 🕒 06 6999 4318; reservations 06 328101 🕒 Tue–Sun 8.30–7.30; closed holidays 🚌 All services to Piazza Venezia 🖐 Moderate

PALAZZO SPADA
This pretty *palazzo*, with a creamy stucco façade (1556–60), has four rooms where you can admire the 17th- and 18th-century Spada family paintings. Cardinal Spada is portrayed by Guido Reni; there's a fine Borromini *Perspective* and works by Albrecht Dürer, Andrea del Sarto and others.
✠ F6 ✉ Piazza Capo di Ferro 13–Vicolo del Polverone 15b 🕿 06 687 4893/4896 or 06 683 2409 🕒 Tue–Sat 8.30–7.30 🚌 H, 8, 63, 630, 780 to Via Arenula 🖐 Moderate

SANT'AGOSTINO
One of the first Renaissance churches in Rome, Sant'Agostino still maintains its Latin-cross plan with apse, chapels and dome. Even if 19th-century additions have ruined its elegance, it is still worth visiting to see the works of Caravaggio, Raphael and other fine artists. The first chapel on the left contains Caravaggio's magnificent *Madonna di Loreto*.
✠ F5 ✉ Piazza di Sant'Agostino 🕒 Daily 8–12, 4.30–7.30 🚌 116 to Via Zanardelli; 30, 40, 46, 62, 63, 64, 70 to Largo di Torre Argentina; 30, 70, 87, 130, 186 to Corso del Rinascimento

The perspectival gallery in the Palazzo Spada

Sant'Agostino, one of Rome's earliest Renaissance churches

The Medieval City

Explore the tangle of streets around some of Rome's most popular piazzas, taking in some of the best-known sights along the way.

DISTANCE: 2.5km (1.5 miles)   **ALLOW:** 2 hours

START

CAMPO DE' FIORI (▷ 48)
🚌 F6 🚎 40, 60, 62, 116 and other services to Corso Vittorio Emanuele II

END

PIAZZA DELLA ROTONDA
🚌 F5 🚎 116, 116T to Piazza della Rotonda

① Walk east on Via dei Giubbonari and take the third right, Via d'Arco del Monte. Continue down Via dei Pettinari and and right through the arch into Via Giulia.

② Take the fourth right opposite the church with the skull-adorned façade and admire Piazza Farnese before following Vicolo Gallo back into Campo de' Fiori.

③ Take Via dei Cappellari out of the campo and go left on Via del Pellegrino and then right on Via dei Banchi Vecchi. Cross Corso Vittorio Emanuele II into Via Banco Santo Spirito, then go immediately right on Via del Governo Vecchio.

④ Continue to the end to visit Piazza Navona (▷ 49). Or explore the tangle of lovely streets to the west of this piazza by turning sixth left on Vicolo del Corallo to Piazza del Fico.

⑧ Otherwise, go north on Via della Scrofa, then right on Via Stelletta to Piazza Campo Marzio. Turn right on Via Uffici del Vicario, then right on Via Maddalena to Piazza della Rotonda.

⑦ Take the southeast corner of Piazza Sant'Apollinare into Piazza Sant' Agostino to see the church (▷ 52). Go past the church and left into Via della Scrofa. Turn right on Via della Scrofa and cross Largo Toniolo to see the Caravaggios in San Luigi dei Francesi.

⑥ Turn left to look at antiques shops on Via dei Coronari, or right and cross Piazza di Tor Sanguigna, and then left into Piazza Sant' Apollinare, to the Palazzo Altemps (▷ 42–43).

⑤ Take Via della Fossa east out of Piazza del Fico and turn left on Via del Parione, then left on Vicolo delle Volpe to Via dei Coronari.

Shopping

AI MONASTERI

This unusual, large and rather dark old shop sells the products of seven Italian monasteries, from honeys, wines, natural preserves and liqueurs to herbal cures and elixirs.

✚ F5 ✉ Piazza Cinque Lune 76 ☎ 06 6880 2783 ⏰ Fri–Wed 9–1, 4.30–7.30, Thu 9–1; closed 1st week of Sep

ANTICA LIBRERIA CROCE

This primarily Italian bookshop, with some titles in English, specializes in books on all aspects of Classical and contemporary art and photography. Over two floors; from time to time exhibitions are held here.

✚ F6 ✉ Corso Vittorio Emanuele II 56, corner of Corso del Rinascimento ☎ 06 6880 2269 ⏰ Mon–Sat 10–8, Sun 10–1.30, 4–8.30

BASSETTI

Central shop with a dazzling collection of quality Italian silks and other luxurious fabrics, plus everyday materials.

✚ E5 ✉ Corso Vittorio Emanuele II 73 ☎ 06 689 2326 ⏰ Tue–Sat 9–7.30 (Jul–end Aug 9–1, 4–6), Mon 4–6 (hours can vary)

CAMPO DE' FIORI

This picturesque market is in a pretty, central square. Fruit and vegetables dominate, but you can also buy fish, flowers and beans.

✚ F6 ✉ Piazza Campo de' Fiori ⏰ Mon–Sat 7am–1.30pm

CULTI

Shop near Piazza Navona packed with linens, well-designed kitchen utensils, plates, glasses, vases, towels, sheets and a host of other articles for the home.

SHOPPING AREAS

Most of the city's quality and specialty shops are concentrated in specific areas. Via Condotti and its surrounding grid of streets (Via Frattina, Via Borgognana and Via Bocca di Leone) contain most of the big names in men's and women's fashion, accessories, jewellery and luxury goods. In nearby Via del Babuino and Via Margutta, the emphasis is on top antiques, paintings, sculpture and modern glassware and lighting. Via della Croce, which runs south from Piazza di Spagna, is known for its food shops, while Via del Corso, which bisects the northern half of central Rome, is home to bargain mid-range clothes, shoes and accessories shops. For inexpensive shops visit Via del Tritone and Via Nazionale. Nice areas to browse for antiques, even if you are not buying, include Via Giulia, Via dei Coronari, Via dell'Orso, Via dei Soldati and Via del Governo Vecchio.

✚ F5 ✉ Via della Vetrina 16a ☎ 06 683 2180 ⏰ Tue–Sat 10–1.30, 4–7.30, Mon 4–7.30

ENOTECA AL GOCCETTO

Wines from all over Italy are sold in this old bishop's *palazzo*, complete with original floors and wooden ceiling.

✚ E5 ✉ Via dei Banchi Vecchi 14 ☎ 06 686 4268 ⏰ Mon–Sat 11.30–2, 7–11, closed 3 weeks in Aug

ETHIC

One of many inexpensive stores with good mid-range fashion just east of Campo de' Fiori.

✚ F6 ✉ Piazza Benedetto Cairoli 11–12 ☎ 06 6830 1063 ⏰ Tue–Sat 10–8, Sun–Mon 12–8

FABINDIA

www.fabindia.it

Facing the Ponte Sant'Angelo is this delightful emporium selling Indian fabrics, scarves and garments, all hand-woven and made in Indian villages. The company is devoted to developing fair and equitable relationships with the producers. The style is both traditional and more contemporary.

✚ E5 ✉ Via del Banco di Santo Spirito 40 ☎ 06 6889 1230 ⏰ Mon–Sat 10–1.30, 3–7.30

FELTRINELLI

An Italy-wide bookshop chain with well-designed

shelves displaying a broad range of Italian titles, and usually a reasonable choice of French-German- and English-language books.

🚹 F6 ⊠ Largo di Torre Argentina 7–10 ☎ 06 6866 3001 🕙 Mon–Sat 9–8, Sun 10–1.30, 4–7.30

🚹 G3 ⊠ Via del Babuino 39–41 ☎ 06 3600 1873 🕙 Mon–Sat 9–8, Sun 10–1.30, 4–7.30

🚹 J4 ⊠ Via Vittorio Emanuele II Orlando 78–81/84 ☎ 06 484 430 or 06 487 0171 🕙 Mon– Sat 9–8, Sun 10–1.30, 4–7.30

HOUSE & KITCHEN

More traditional than Spazio Sette (▷ below). This shop sells a range of household goods, notably a selection of kitchen utensils and kitchenware.

🚹 G6 ⊠ Via del Plebiscito 103 ☎ 06 679 4208 🕙 Mon–Sat 9.30–8, Sun 10.30–2.30, 4–8; closed Sun in Jul and Aug

MARIA GRAZIA LUFFARELLI

Bright watercolour landscapes of hills, sea and sun. Prices range from very low to moderate for original works by the eponymous artist. Also on sale is a lovely range of Rome watercolour reproductions in postcard format, plus prints of Luffarelli's work mounted on brightly painted tables.

🚹 E5 ⊠ Via dei Banchi Vecchi 29 ☎ 06 683 2494 🕙 Mon–Sat 11–8

MONDELLO OTTICA

www.mondelloottica.it Eyewear with a difference: This minimalist boutique has regular installations by local artists. Prices may be higher than average, but the glasses are superlative in quality and sheer chic. All have that little extra something special that makes the price worth paying.

🚹 E5 ⊠ Vial del Pellegrino 98 ☎ 06 686 1955 🕙 Tue–Sat 9.30–1, 4–7.30

ORNAMENTUM

A beautiful shop selling silks and other sumptuous fabrics, tassels, brocades and other furnishing accessories.

🚹 E5 ⊠ Via dei Coronari 227 ☎ 06 687 6849 🕙 Tue–Fri 9–1, 4–7.30, Sat 9–1, Mon 4–7.30; closed Aug

GIFTS WITH A TWIST

For a souvenir with a difference, visit the extraordinary shops on Via dei Cestari, just south of the Pantheon, which specialize in all sorts of religious clothes, candles and vestments. Crucifixes, rosaries, statues of saints and other religious souvenirs can be found in shops on Via di Porta Angelica near the Vatican. Alternatively, visit the Farmacia Santa Maria della Scala (⊠ Piazza Santa Maria della Scala), an 18th-century monastic pharmacy that sells herbal remedies.

PIAZZA COPPELLE

This tiny, attractive local food market is an oasis among the cars and tourists. Close to the Pantheon.

🚹 F5 ⊠ Piazza Coppelle 🕙 Mon–Sat 7am–1pm

POGGI

Vivid pigments, lovely papers and exquisitely soft brushes have been on sale at Poggi's since 1825. The second shop almost opposite sells high-quality paper.

🚹 G5 ⊠ Via del Gesù 74–5 ☎ 06 678 4477 🕙 Mon–Sat 9–1, 4–7.30

🚹 G5 ⊠ Via Piè di Marmo 40–1 ☎ 06 6830 8014 🕙 Mon–Fri 9–1, 4–7.30, Sat 9–1

IL SIGILLO

Close to the Pantheon, this little shop specializes in fine pens, hand-printed stationery and a wide variety of objects covered in marbled paper.

🚹 F5 ⊠ Via della Guglia 69 ☎ 06 678 9667 🕙 Daily 11–8

SPAZIO SETTE

Housed in a 17th-century cardinal's palace, this is one of the few stores in Rome that will make even the most hardened shopper salivate over furnishings for the kitchen, living room and bathroom.

🚹 F6 ⊠ Via dei Barbieri 7 ☎ 06 6880 4261 🕙 Tue–Sat 9.30–1, 3.30–7.30, Mon 3.30–7.30

Entertainment and Nightlife

ANIMA

At the heart of a small buzzing nightlife area, Anima is a welcoming bar and club that plays an eclectic assortment of music and attracts a clientele of all ages and types.

+ F5 **⊠** Via Santa Maria dell'Anima **☎** 06 6889 2806 **◎** Daily 12am–4am **🚌** 30, 70, 87 and other services to Corso del Rinascimento

ASSOCIAZIONE MUSICALE ROMANA

www.assmusrom.it

Stages a summer season of chamber recitals at a number of venues, including the French Academy in the Villa Medici.

+ G3 **⊠** Via Gregorio 216 **☎** 06 3936 6322

BEVITORIA

Friendlier and more intimate than most large or touristy bars on Piazza Navona. Primarily a wine bar (the cellar is part of Domitian's former stadium). Gets busy.

+ F5 **⊠** Piazza Navona 72 **☎** 06 6880 1022 **◎** Daily 11am–1am **🚌** 46, 62, 64 to Corso Vittorio Emanuele II or 30, 70, 81, 87, 116 to Corso del Rinascimento

CUL DE SAC

An established informal wine bar near Piazza Navona with pine tables and a big marble bar. More than 1,400 wines, plus snacks, light meals and cheese and salami from every region in Italy.

+ F5 **⊠** Piazza Pasquino 73 **☎** 06 6880 1094 **◎** Daily 12–4pm, 6–12.30 **🚌** 46, 62, 64 to Corso Vittorio Emanuele II

IL GONFALONE

A small but prestigious company that hosts chamber music and other small-scale recitals.

+ E5 **⊠** Oratorio del Gonfalone, Via del Gonfalone 32a; Information **⊠** Vicolo della Scimmia 1b **☎** 06 687 5952; www.romeguide.it/musica **◎** Concerts Oct–Jun, call for times; box office Mon–Fri 9am–1pm, day of concert 9–9 **🚌** 46, 62, 64 to Corso Vittorio Emanuele II or 23, 116, 280 to Lungotevere di Sangallo

MAD JACK'S

www.madjacks.com

This Irish pub will suit

WHAT TO DRINK

The most inexpensive way to drink beer in Italy is from the keg (*alla spina*). Measures are *piccola*, *media* and *grande* (usually 33cl, 50cl and a litre respectively). Foreign canned or bottled beers (*in lattina* or *in bottiglia*) are expensive. Italian brands like Peroni are a little less expensive: a Peroncino (25cl bottle) is a good thirst-quencher. Aperitifs (*aperitivi*) include popular non-alcoholic drinks like Aperol, Crodino and San Pellegrino bitter. A glass of red or white wine is *un bicchiere di vino rosso/bianco*.

those looking for a festive place in which to pass the night hours. The music is loud and drinks are flowing.

+ F6 **⊠** Via Arenula 20 **☎** 06 6880 8223 **◎** Daily 11.30am–2am **🚌** 40, 64 to Largo di Torre Argentina **🎟** Free

IL PICCOLO

Intimate wine bar close to Piazza Navona, ideal for a romantic interlude.

+ E5 **⊠** Via del Governo Vecchio 74–5 **☎** 06 6880 1746 **◎** Daily noon–2am **🚌** 46, 62, 64 to Corso Vittorio Emanuele II

TRINITY COLLEGE

English and Irish-style pubs are all the rage—this is one of the better ones. Its serves inexpensive food as well as Guinness.

+ G5 **⊠** Via del Collegio Romano **☎** 06 678 6472 **◎** Daily noon–3am **🚌** 62, 63, 85, 95, 117, 119 to Via del Corso and all services to Piazza Venezia

LA VINERIA REGGIO

The quainter side of nighttime drinking. Fusty and old-fashioned inside, with characters to match; tables on the city's most evocative square. Also try the popular Drunken Ship pub virtually next door.

+ F6 **⊠** Campo de' Fiori 15 **☎** 06 6880 3268 **◎** Mon–Sat 8.30am–2am, Sun 5pm–2am **🚌** 46, 62, 64 to Corso Vittorio Emanuele II, 116 to Via Baullari or 70, 81, 87 to Corso del Rinascimento

Restaurants

PRICES

Prices are approximate, based on a 3-course meal for one person.

€€€	over €50
€€	€30–€50
€	under €30

ANTICA BIRRERIA FRATELLI TEMPERA (€)

Ideal for a simple lunch or dinner. Original art nouveau interior and a large beer hall.

🚼 G5 ⊠ Via di San Marcello 19 ☎ 06 678 6203 🕐 Mon–Sat 12–12 🚌 44, 46, 64, 70, 87 and all other buses to Piazza Venezia

IL BACARO (€€)

www.ilbacaro.com

Tiny but gracious restaurant. It can be noisy, but the light, modern pan-Italian cooking is great.

🚼 F5 ⊠ Via degli Spagnoli 27, near Piazza delle Coppelle ☎ 06 686 4110 or 06 687 2554 🕐 Mon–Sat 8am–11.30pm; closed Aug 🚇 Spagna 🚌 119

BAFFETTO (€)

A tiny, hole-in-the wall classic that has retained its atmosphere and low prices. Expect to wait for a table.

🚼 E5 ⊠ Via del Governo Vecchio 114 ☎ 06 686 1617 🕐 Daily 6.30 –1am; closed Aug 🚌 46, 62, 64 to Corso Vittorio Emanuele II

BAR DELLA PACE (€)

Extremely trendy bar, which is quieter by day, when you can eat outside or enjoy the 19th-century mahogany interior.

🚼 F5 ⊠ Via della Pace 3, off Piazza Navona ☎ 06 686 1216 🕐 Daily 9am–2am; closed Mon am 🚌 30, 70, 87, 116 to Corso del Rinascimento

BRAMANTE (€€€)

The setting of this chic restaurant, complete with an art nouveau window, could scarcely be bettered: It's on one of the city's most prestigious and beautiful baroque squares, Piazza Navona. Inside, you could be in a Tuscan villa, softly lit with oil lamps; the walls are frescoed with local scenes and classical music plays. The food is not the most imaginative

THE MENU

Starters are called antipasti; first course (soup, pasta or risotto) is *il primo*; and main meat and fish dishes are *il secondo*. Salads (*insalata*) and vegetables (*contorni*) are ordered (and often eaten) separately. Desserts are *dolci*, with cheese (*formaggio*) or fruit (*frutta*) to follow. If no menu card is offered, ask for *la lista* or *il menù*. A set-price menu (*un menù turistico*) may seem good value, but portions are usually small and the food is invariably poor—usually just spaghetti with a tomato sauce, followed by a piece of chicken and fruit.

but good and the service is first class.

🚼 F5 ⊠ Via della Pace 25 ☎ 06 6880 3916 🕐 Mon–Sat 6.30pm–2am, Sun 12.30–2pm (summer only) 🚌 46, 62, 64, 87, 116, 492 to Corso del Rinascimento

CAFFÈ FARNESE (€)

Quieter and more elegant than the bars on the nearby Campo de' Fiori. Serves cakes, ice creams and light snacks as well as drinks. Also has tables on the cobbled street outside.

🚼 E6 ⊠ Via dei Baullari 106–7, at Piazza Farnese ☎ 06 6880 2125 🕐 Daily 7am–2am 🚌 8, 46, 62, 64

IL CONVIVIO (€€€)

www.ilconviviotroiani.com

The Troiani brothers from Italy's Marche region have created a tranquil little restaurant with a reputation for innovative and subtle tasting modern dishes.

🚼 F4 ⊠ Vicolo dei Soldati 31 ☎ 06 686 9432 🕐 Mon–Sat dinner only 8–10.30 🚌 30, 70, 87, 116, 492 to Corso del Rinascimento

CORALLO (€)

This stylish pizzeria is convenient to Piazza Navona. Full meals also available.

🚼 F5 ⊠ Via del Corallo 10, off Via del Governo Vecchio ☎ 06 6830 7703 🕐 Mon 7.30pm–11.30pm, Tue–Sun 12–2.30, 7–1am; closed 1 week in Aug 🚌 46, 62, 64 to Corso Vittorio Emanuele II

CICCIA BOMBA (€€)

An excellent option amid the plethora of restaurants around Piazza Navona. Simple wooden tables, efficient service, and good Roman food at good prices for this area. 🚇 E5 ✉ Via dell Governo Vecchio 76 ☎ 06 6880 2108 🕐 Thu–Tue 12.30–3, 7.30–11.30; closed 2 weeks in Aug 🚌 All services to Corso del Rinascimento or Corso Vittorio Emanuele II

DA FRANCESCO (€)

A simple restaurant near Piazza Navona, which over the years has never lost its appeal, thanks to a warm, friendly atmosphere, good food and low prices. No reservations so arrive early to be sure of a place. 🚇 E5 ✉ Piazza del Fico ☎ 06 686 4009 🕐 Wed–Mon 12–3, 7–1, Tue 7pm–1am 🚌 64 and other services to Chiesa Nuova on Corso Vittorio Emanuele II

DITIRAMBO (€€)

www.ristoranteditirambo.it Downtown *trattoria* that far transcends the tourist menu, even satisfying the difficult-to-please *bel mondo* of Rome. The kitchen uses organic ingredients, and produces homemade bread, pasta and desserts. Reservations essential. 🚇 F6 ✉ Piazza della Cancelleria 74 ☎ 06 687 1626 🕐 Tue–Sun 1–3, 7.30–11.30, Mon 8pm–11.30pm; closed Aug

🚌 46, 62, 64, 87, 116, 492 to Corso Vittorio Emanuele II

DUR FILETTARO A SANTA BARBARA (€)

At this tiny place with Formica tables you wash down cod with plenty of beer or crisp local wine. 🚇 F6 ✉ Largo dei Librari 88, off Via dei Giubbonari ☎ 06 686 4018 🕐 Mon–Sat 5.30–11; closed Aug and 1 week Dec–Jan 🚌 H, 8, 63, 630, 780 to Via Arenula

GELATERIA DELLA PALMA (€)

A big, brash place just behind the Pantheon. Cakes and chocolates, plus over 100 flavours of ice cream—many of them a little wild. 🚇 F5 ✉ Via della Maddalena 20 ☎ 06 6880

THE BILL

The bill (check), *il conto*, usually includes extras such as *servizio* (service). Iniquitous cover charges (*pane e coperto*) have now been outlawed, but some restaurants still try to get round the regulations. Only pay for bread (*pane*) if you have asked for it. Proper receipts—not a scrawled piece of paper—must be given by law. If you receive a scrap of paper, which is more likely in a pizzeria, and have doubts about the total, be sure to ask for a proper receipt (*una fattura* or *una ricevuta*).

6752 🕐 Daily 8am–midnight 🚌 116 to Piazza della Rotonda

GIOLITTI (€)

For years Giolitti was the king of Roman ice cream. Standards have slipped slightly, but the ice cream is still excellent value. 🚇 F5 ✉ Via Uffici del Vicario 40 ☎ 06 699 1243 🕐 Mon–Fri, Sun 7am–12.30am, Sat 7am–2am 🚌 119 to Piazza della Rotonda or 62, 80, 81, 85, 95, 117, 119, 160, 175 and other services to Via del Corso

GRAPPOLO D'ORO (€)

Unspoiled *trattoria* loved by locals and foreign residents for decades. The menu has *pasta all' Amatriciana* and *scaloppine* any way you like. 🚇 F6 ✉ Piazza della Cancelleria 80 ☎ 06 689 7080 🕐 Daily 12.30–2.30, 7.30–10.30; closed lunch Tue–Fri in winter 🚌 46, 62, 64 to Corso Vittorio Emanuele II

'GUSTO (€€)

A chic, modern restaurant on two levels where you can eat pizzas, salads and other light meals downstairs or fuller meals upstairs. There is also a good kitchenware shop. 🚇 F3 ✉ Piazza Augusto Imperatore 9 ☎ 06 322 6273 🕐 Daily 1–3, 7.30–1 🚌 117, 119 to Via del Corso

LATTERIA DEL GALLO (€)

Marble tables and 1940s decor. Try the big, sticky cakes and steaming

hot chocolate.

➕ E6 ✉ Vicolo del Gallo 4 ☎ 06 686 5091 🕐 Thu–Tue 8.30–2, 5–midnight 🚌 46, 62, 64 to Corso Vittorio Emanuele II

L'EAU VIVE (€€)

Expect a bizarre dining experience here. The predominantly French food is served by nuns. Politicians, celebrities and locals come to enjoy the food and the beautiful 16th-century frescoed dining rooms.

➕ F5 ✉ Via Monterone 85 ☎ 06 654 1095 or 06 6880 1095 🕐 Mon–Sat 12.30–3.30, 7.30–10; closed Aug 🚌 8, 46, 62, 63, 64, 70, 87, 186, 492 to Largo di Torre Argentina

LA ROSETTA (€€€)

An exclusive fish and seafood restaurant whose popularity means reservations are a must.

➕ F5 ✉ Via della Rosetta 8–9 ☎ 06 686 1002 🕐 Mon–Sat 1–3, 8–11.30; closed 2 weeks in Aug 🚌 119 to Piazza della Rotonda or 70, 87, 90 to Corso del Rinascimento

SALOTTO 42

Warm and relaxed place for drinks or light meals, especially at lunch (the kitchen closes at 9.30pm). In the evening it transforms into a stylish cocktail bar.

➕ G5 ✉ Piazza di Pietro 42 ☎ 06 678 5804 Tues–Sun 🕐 10am–2am (earlier on Sun) 🚌 C3, 62, 63, 85, 91,

117, 119 and other services to Via del Corso

SANT' EUSTACHIO (€)

Excellent coffee served in a pleasant interior and tables outside.

➕ F5 ✉ Piazza Sant' Eustachio 82 ☎ 06 6880 2048 🕐 Daily 8.30am–1am 🚌 119 to Piazza della Rotonda or 30, 70, 87, 116 to Corso del Rinascimento

LA TAZZA D'ORO (€)

The 'Cup of Gold' sells only coffee, and probably the city's best espresso.

➕ F5 ✉ Via degli Orfani 84 ☎ 06 678 9792 🕐 Mon–Sat 7am–8pm 🚌 119 to Piazza della Rotonda or 30, 70, 87, 116, 186 to Corso del Rinascimento

THIEN KIM (€)

More adventurous Romans have been visiting this calm and

UNUSUAL WAITRESSES

You are served at the L'Eau Vive by nuns from a third world order known as the Vergini Laiche Cristiane di Azione Cattolica Missionaria per Mezzo del Lavoro (Christian Virgins of Catholic Missionary Action through Work). With restaurants in several parts of the world, their aim is to spread the message of Christianity through the medium of French food. To this end, dining is interrupted by prayers each evening at 9.

---

courteous restaurant for Thai food since 1976. Very good value.

➕ E6 ✉ Via Giulia 201 ☎ 06 6830 7832 🕐 Mon–Sat 7.30–10.30 🚌 46, 64 to Corso Vittorio Emanuele II

TRE SCALINI (€)

Known for its chocolate-studded *tartufo* (the best chocolate-chip ice cream).

➕ F5 ✉ Piazza Navona 28–32 ☎ 06 6880 1996 🕐 Daily Thu–Tue 8am–1am 🚌 30, 70, 87, 116 and other services to Corso del Rinascimento

TUCCI (€)

You can sit here for hours facing Bernini's Fontana dei Quattro Fiumi, but watch your bill.

➕ F5 ✉ Piazza Navona 94–100 ☎ 06 686 1547 🕐 Wed–Mon 8.30am–12.30am 🚌 46, 62, 64 to Corso Vittorio Emanuele II or 30, 70, 87, 116 to Corso del Rinascimento

VECCHIA ROMA (€€€)

In a pretty piazza and perfect for an alfresco meal on a summer evening. Although the 18th-century interior is also captivating, prices are rather high for what is only straightforward and reliable Roman cooking.

➕ F6 ✉ Piazza Campitelli 18 ☎ 06 686 4604 🕐 Mon, Tue, Thu–Sun 1–3, 8–11; closed 3 weeks in Aug 🚌 All services to Via Arenula or Piazza Venezia

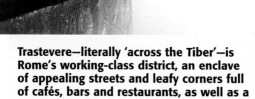

Trastevere—literally 'across the Tiber'—is Rome's working-class district, an enclave of appealing streets and leafy corners full of cafés, bars and restaurants, as well as a handful of churches and galleries.

Trastevere and the South

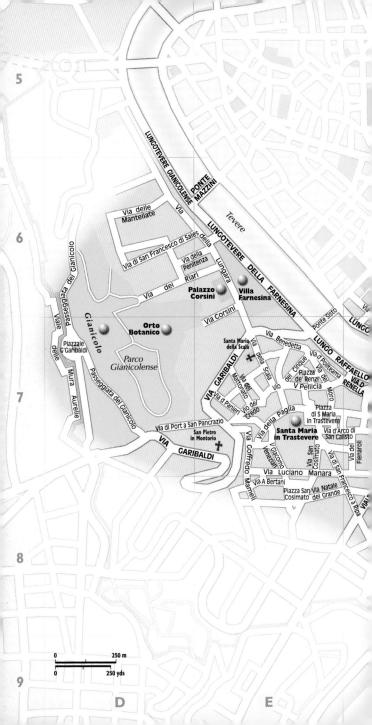

5

6

7

8

9

Via delle Mantellate

Via di San Francesco di Sales

Via della Penitenza

Via del Riari

LUNGOTEVERE GIANICOLENSE

PONTE MAZZINI

Tevere

LUNGOTEVERE DELLA FARNESINA

Ponte Sisto

LUNGO

LUNGO RAFFAELLO

Via

Lungara

Palazzo Corsini

Villa Farnesina

Via Corsini

Via Benedetta

Santa Maria della Scala

Via della Scala

Via d Politeama

VIA D RENELLA

Gianicolo

Passeggiata del Gianicolo

Viale delle Mura Aurelie

Piazzale G Garibaldi

Orto Botanico

Parco Gianicolense

Passeggiata del Gianicolo

Via di Port a San Pancrazio

San Pietro in Montorio

VIA GARIBALDI

VIA GARIBALDI

Via del Mattonato

Via d Panien

Vio del Credo

Via del Cinque

Via del Moro

Piazza de' Renzi

V Pellicia

Piazza di S Maria in Trastevere

Santa Maria in Trastevere

Via della Paglia

Via Goffredo Mamell

Giacomo Venezian

Via San Cosimato

Via San Francesco a Rina

Via d'Arco di San Calisto

Via del Fienaroli

Via Luciano Manara

Via A Bertani

Piazza San Cosimato

Via Natale del Grande

VIA

0   250 m

0   250 yds

D   **E**

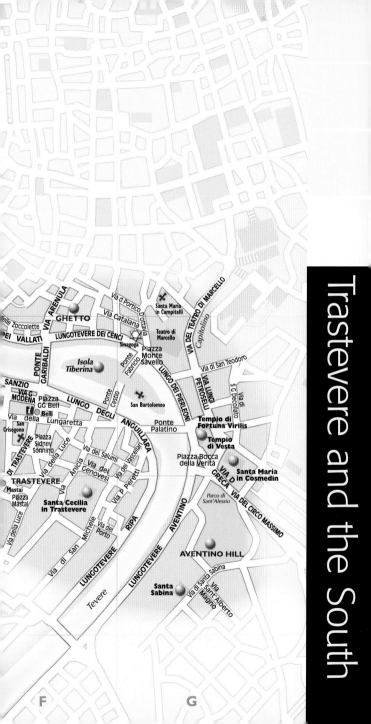

VIA ARENULA

GHETTO

Via d Portico d'Ottavia

Santa Maria
in Campitelli

Via Catalana

Teatro di
Marcello

VIA DEL TEATRO DI MARCELLO

PONTE GARIBALDI

elle Zoccolette

DEI VALLATI

LUNGOTEVERE DEI CENCI

Sinagoga

Piazza
Monte
Savello

Capitolino

Isola
Tiberina

Ponte Fabricio

LUNGO DEI PIERLEONI

Via di San Teodoro

SANZIO

VIA G
MODENA

Piazza
GG Bell

Ponte Cestio

LUNGO DEGLI

San Bartolomeo

Via di S C Decollato

VIA LUNGARINA PETROSELLI

Belli

Via
della
Lungaretta

ANGUILLARA

Ponte
Palatino

Tempio di
Fortuna Virilis

Via
San
Crisogono

Piazza
Sidney
Sonnino

DI TRASTEVERE

Via del Salumi

Via della Luce

Via del Vascellari

Piazza Bocca
della Verità

Tempio
di Vesta

Santa Maria
in Cosmedin

VIA D
GRECA

VIA DEL CIRCO MASSIMO

TRASTEVERE

Mastai
Piazza
Mastai

Santa Cecilia
in Trastevere

Via
Anicia

Via del
Genovesi

Via P. Peretti

RIPA

Parco di
Sant'Alessio

AVENTINO

Via della Luce

Via del
Porto

Via di San Michele

LUNGOTEVERE

LUNGOTEVERE

AVENTINO HILL

Tevere

Santa
Sabina

Via di Santa Sabina

Via
Sant'Alberto
Magno

F

G

Santa Maria in Trastevere

HIGHLIGHTS

- Romanesque campanile
- Façade mosaics
- Portico
- Ceiling, designed by Domenichino
- Cosmati marble pavement
- Wall tabernacle by Mino del Reame (central nave)
- Byzantine mosaics, upper apse
- Mosaics: *Life of the Virgin* (lower apse)
- *Madonna della Clemenza* in Cappella Altemps
- Cappella Avila: baroque chapel

TIP

- Visit in the evening, then have a drink in one of the outdoor cafés, from where you can appreciate the lit piazza and basilica.

One of the most memorable sights of night-time Rome is the 12th-century gold mosaics on the façade of Santa Maria in Trastevere, their floodlit glow casting a gentle light over the piazza below.

Early church Santa Maria in Trastevere is among the oldest officially sanctioned places of worship in Rome. It was reputedly founded in AD222, allegedly on the spot where a fountain of olive oil had sprung from the earth on the day of Christ's birth (symbolizing the coming of the grace of God). Much of the present church was built in the 12th century during the reign of Innocent II, a member of the Papareschi, a prominent Trastevere family. Inside, the main colonnade of the nave is composed of reused and ancient Roman columns. The portico, containing fragments of Roman reliefs and

A fountain graces the piazza outside the church (far left). The apse mosaics are a highlight of this medieval church (left, bottom right and middle). Night time in Piazza di Santa Maria in Trastevere (right). Twenty-two columns from ancient monuments divide the nave from the aisles (bottom left)

inscriptions and medieval remains, was added in 1702 by Carlo Fontana, who was responsible for the fountain that graces the adjoining piazza.

Mosaics The façade mosaics probably date from the mid-12th century, and depict the Virgin and Child with 10 lamp-carrying companions. Long believed to portray the parable of the Wise and Foolish Virgins, their subject matter is contested, as several 'virgins' appear to be men and only two are carrying unlighted lamps (not the five of the parable). The mosaics of the upper apse inside the church, devoted to the glorification of the Virgin, date from the same period and are Byzantine-influenced works by Greek or Greek-trained craftsmen. Those below, depicting scenes from the life of the Virgin (1291), are by the mosaicist and fresco painter Pietro Cavallini.

THE BASICS

✚ E7

✉ Piazza Santa Maria in Trastevere

☎ 06 361 0836 or 06 581 4802

🕐 Daily 7.45–8/9 (may close 12.30–3.30 in winter)

🚌 H, 8, 780 Viale di Trastevere, 125 to Via Manara or 23, 280 to Lungotevere Raffaello Sanzio

♿ Wheelchair accessible

🎟 Free

Villa Farnesina

The Salone delle Prospettive (left). Villa Farnesina's gardens, ideal for a walk (right)

THE BASICS

www.francopanini.it

+ E6
✉ Via della Lungara 230
☎ 06 6802 7268
🕐 Mon–Sat 9–1
🚌 23, 125, 280 to Lungotevere della Farnesina
♿ Moderate

HIGHLIGHTS

● The Loggia of Cupid and Psyche, decorated with frescos by Raphael
● Sodoma's Scenes from the *Life of Alexander the Great*
● Salone delle Prospettive
● Peruzzi's *trompe l'oeil* views of Rome
● The gardens

This is one of the most intimate and charming of all Rome's grand houses, known as much for its peaceful gardens as for its beautifully decorated interior, which contains works commissioned from Raphael and other artists by the villa's original owner, Agostino Chigi.

All to impress In 1508, Agostino Chigi, a wealthy banker from Siena, commissioned Baldasssare Puruzzi to build him a suburban villa. Here, Chigi entertained artists, princes and cardinals. His banquets were memorable: After the meal, Chigi would have the gold and silver dishes thrown into the Tiber to impress his guests with his wealth. What they did not know was that the plates were caught by safety nets and returned to the kitchens. In 1580, the villa was bought by the Farnese family, and it has been known as Villa Farnesina ever since.

Lots to admire On the ground floor are the Loggia of Galatea, with a much admired fresco by Raphael of the *Triumph of Galatea*, and the Loggia of Cupid and Psyche, frescoed to Raphael's designs by some of his pupils (including the future star of Mannerist painting, Giulio Romano). On the upper floor is the beautiful Salone delle Prospettive, with a fresco by Baldassare Peruzzi of a *trompe l'oeil* colonnade through which can be seen rural landscapes, villages and a town. Finally, visit Chigi's former bed chamber, decorated with an erotic fresco, *The Wedding Night of Alexander the Great and Roxane*, by Il Sodoma.

More to See

AVENTINO HILL
The most southerly of Rome's seven hills and one of the most beautiful quarters. Here the traffic and chaos of the city are left far behind, replaced by peaceful churches, charming cloisters, beautiful gardens and panoramic views over Trastevere and St. Peter's.

✚ G8 🚇 Circo Massimo 🚌 C3, 81, 160, 628, 715 to Via del Circo Massimo

GHETTO
This picturesque place, its narrow streets full of Jewish restaurants, pastry shops and workshops, is still a meeting place for the Roman-Jewish community. The Synagogue, built in 1904 overlooking the Tiber, its great dome visible from all over the city, houses the Jewish Museum.

✚ F6 ☎ Synagogue 06 6400 0661
🕐 Mon–Thu 9–4.30, Fri 9–1.30, Sun 9–12.30
🚌 23, 63, 280, 630, 780 💰 Moderate

GIANICOLO
Not one of Rome's original seven hills, but the best view of Rome has to be from the Janiculum Hill. There are spectacular views all the way up from the Passeggiata del Gianicolo, a fine avenue that runs around the hill. En route visit the little Tempietto designed by Bramante in 1508, and the church of San Pietro in Montorio.

✚ D7 ✉ Passeggiata del Gianicolo
🕐 Tempietto Tue–Sun 9.30–12.30, 4–6 (2–4 Nov–end Apr); church daily 9–12, 4–6
🚌 44, 75, 115, 125 to the Gianicolo or Via Garibaldi

ISOLA TIBERINA
This small island in the Tiber with its medieval buildings and Roman bridges, feels like a safe haven, protected from the chaos of the city. The island is on a volcanic rock and its shape resembles that of a ship. Two bridges join the Isola Tiberina to the riverbanks: the Ponte Cestio dates back to the first century BC, and leads to Trastevere; while the Ponte Fabricio, built in 62BC, the only Roman bridge to survive intact, joins the island to the Ghetto.

✚ F7 🚌 H, 23, 63, 280, 780 to Lungotevere dei Cenci and all services to Via Arenula and Largo di Torre Argentina

From Gianicolo a panorama of Rome opens up before you

The narrow streets of the Ghetto Quarter

ORTO BOTANICO

Trastevere has few open spaces, so these university gardens and their 7,000 or so botanical species provide a welcome oasis of green shade.

⊕ D7 ⊠ Largo Cristina di Svezia 24, off Via Corsini ☎ 06 4991 7107 🕒 Tue–Sat 9.30–6.30 (5.30 in winter). Closed holidays and Aug 🚌 23, 280 to Lungotevere Farnesina 💷 Moderate

PALAZZO CORSINI

Though in a separate building, this gallery is part of the Palazzo Barberini's Galleria Nazionale. Originally part of the Corsini family's 17th-century collection, it became state property in 1883. Pictures from the 16th to 18th century hang alongside bronzes and sculptures in a series of elegant rooms.

⊕ E6 ⊠ Via della Lungara 10 ☎ 06 6880 2323, reservations 06 328 101; www.ticketeria.it 🕒 Tue–Fri entrance at 9.30, 11, 12.30, Sat–Sun 8.30–1.20 🚌 23, 280, 870 to Lungotevere Farnesina 💷 Moderate

SANTA CECILIA IN TRASTEVERE

Enter the church through a delightful courtyard, with a portico supported by old granite columns and a lily garden with a central fountain. Next you pass a façade designed by Ferdinando Fuga in 1741. Crypt excavations and splendid 9th-century apse mosaics depicting Jesus with saints Paul, Agata, Peter, Paschal, Valeriano and Cecilia are among Santa Cecilia's treasures. Another is the beautiful fresco *Last Judgement* (1293) by Pietro Cavallini, the remains of a medieval masterpiece that once covered the walls of the central nave but was mostly lost in an 18th-century restoration of the church. The fresco was moved to the nuns' choir where it can be viewed.

⊕ F8 ⊠ Piazza di Santa Cecilia 22 ☎ 06 589 9289 or 06 581 2140 🕒 Daily 9.30–12.30, 4–6.30. Cavallini fresco Mon–Sat 10.15–12.15, Sun 11–12.30 🚌 23, 44, 125, 280, 780 to Viale Trastevere or Lungotevere Ripa 💷 Church free; Cavallini fresco inexpensive; crypt expensive

SANTA MARIA IN COSMEDIN

This lovely old medieval church is best known for the Bocca della Verità, a

A charming courtyard fronts Santa Cecilia in Trastevere

Framed by overhanging branches, the ancient bridge linking Isola Tiberina with Trastevere

weather-beaten stone face (of the sea god Oceanus) once used by the ancient Romans as a drain cover. Inside, the church has a beautiful floor, twin pulpits, a bishop's throne and a stone choir screen, all done in fine Cosmati stone inlay. Most date from the 12th century, a little earlier than the impressive *baldacchino* (altar canopy), which was built by Deodato di Cosma in 1294. In a room off the right aisle is a mosaic depicting the *Adoration of the Magi*, almost all that remains of an 8th-century Greek church on the site.

🔒 G7 ✉ Piazza Bocca della Verità 18 ☎ 06 678 1419 🕐 Daily 9–1, 2–7 (6 in winter) 🚌 30, 44, 81, 95, 170 and other routes to Piazza Bocca della Verità or Lungotevere Pierleoni 🖐 Free

SANTA SABINA

The lovely basilica of Santa Sabina, on the Aventine Hill, has kept its original 5th-century early Christian plan almost intact. Next to the church is a beautiful medieval cloister where St. Dominic is said to have planted the first orange tree in Rome, the descendants of which still perfume the monk's garden. At the entrance, behind a front portico, is one of the church's main treasures. The entrance doors are divided into wooden panels, many of them survivors from the 5th-century church, carved with scenes from the Old and New Testaments.

🔒 G8 ✉ Via di Santa Sabina 2 ☎ 06 5794 0660 🕐 Daily 7–12.30, 3.30–7 🚇 Circo Massimo 🚌 C3, 81, 160, 628, 715 to Via del Circo Massimo 🖐 Free

TEMPLES

The Tempio di Vesta and Tempio di Fortuna Virilis are the two best-preserved ancient temples in Rome—all but one of the 20 columns of the former remain standing. Both date from the 2nd century BC, the first named after its resemblance to a similar temple in the Roman Forum. The origins of the second, and the god to whom it was dedicated, remain a mystery.

🔒 G7 ✉ 7 Piazza Bocca della Verità 🚌 C3, H, 81, 160, 175 and other services to Via del Teatro di Marcello and Piazza Bocca della Verità

Inside Santa Sabina, Rome's finest surviving 5th-century Basilica

The Bocca della Verità or 'Mouth of Truth', Santa Maria in Cosmedin

Ghetto to Trastevere

Discover two of Rome's less explored areas, the Ghetto and the Isola Tiberina, before crossing the Tiber to the unspoilt Trastevere.

DISTANCE: 3.5km (2 miles) **ALLOW:** 2–3hours

START

PIAZZA DEL CAMPIDOGLIO
✚ G6 🚌 C3, 40, 63, 70 and all other services to Piazza Venezia

❶ Walk west down the ramp from Piazza del Campidoglio. Cross the road and go down Via d'Aracoeli. Take the second left alley just after the fountain directly into Piazza Margana.

❷ Cross the piazza into Via dei Delfini and follow the street as it curves right into Via dei Funari. Walk along Via dei Funari to Piazza Mattei, home to the Fontana delle Tartarughe (▷ 51).

❸ Continue past the fountain on Via dei Falegnami to busy Via Arenula. Turn left and then immediately left again on Via Santa Maria di Pianto.

❹ Continue along Via Santa Maria di Pianto as it becomes Via del Portico d'Ottavia, named after the gateway on the left. Follow the road as it bears right.

END

PIAZZA DI SANTA MARIA IN TRASTEVERE
✚ E7 🚌 H, 8, 170 to Viale Trastevere or 125 to Via della Scala

❽ In Piazza Sidney Sonnino go left down Via della Lungaretta to Piazza di Santa Maria in Trastevere. Some of the prettiest streets are north of here.

❼ Continue to the church of Santa Cecilia (▷ 68) on your right. With your back to the church, turn left and then first left down Via del Genovesi. Continue straight as this street becomes Via G. C. Santini and turn right at Viale Trastevere.

❻ Go over the Lungotevere and cross the Ponte Fabricio to the Isola Tiberina (▷ 67). Leave the island on the Ponte Cestio and cross over the Lungotevere. Go left and bear right through Piazza Piazza dei Ponziani and right on Via dei Vascellari.

❺ Note the Teatro di Marcello to your left and Rome's main synagogue on your right.

Shopping

ALMAXXURA

A treasure trove of objects is to be found here, all chosen with the greatest care, and of the finest quality. Everything is made in Italy, and some famous names are represented, such as Capodimonte, Marzi and Murano. There is china, porcelain and glass, as well as collectors' dolls and model cars.

➕ F8 ☎ 06 580 6303 ✉ Viale di Trastevere 83 🕐 Mon 4–8, Tue–Sat 10–8

ALMOST CORNER BOOKSHOP

Interesting and unusual selection of books, especially considering the shop's small size. Competitively priced and particularly good on biography and history, with a strong emphasis on Rome and Italy. Helpful and knowledgeable staff.

➕ E7 ✉ Via del Moro 45 ☎ 06 583 6942 🕐 Mon–Sat 10–1.30, 3.30–8, Sun 11–1.30, 3.30–8; closed Sun in Aug

CASIMON

This glorious shop sells a variety of objects in marble, stone, glass and semi-precious stones, from ornamental marble balls and bookends to tables and lampshades.

➕ F7 ✉ Via della Lungaretta 90 ☎ 06 581 4860 🕐 Daily 11am–midnight

LUMIÈRES

Unassuming shop crammed with goods. If an interesting lamp from the French art deco or Italian Liberty periods is what you're after, this is the place to come. Choose from dozens of antique lamps, all fully restored. Or bring your own lamp to be restored by an artisan.

➕ E7 ✉ Vicolo del Cinque 48 ☎ 06 580 3614 🕐 Mon–Sat 10–1, 4–8.30, Sun 4–8

PANDORA

This is an unusual but tasteful store, with a great selection of contemporary Venetian glass items,

LOCAL SHOPPING

Roman supermarkets are few and far between and most food is still bought in tiny local shops known as *alimentari*. Every street of every 'village' or district in the city has one or more of these general shops, a source of everything from olive oil and pasta to candles and corn and bunion treatments. They are also good places to buy picnic provisions—many sell bread and wine—and most have a delicatessen counter that will make you a sandwich (*panino*) from the meats and cheeses on display. For something a little more special, or for food gifts to take home, visit Via della Croce, a street renowned for its wonderful delicatessens.

Italian handmade ceramics, ethnic and handmade jewellery, small antique pieces, and accessories such as scarves and bags.

➕ E7 ✉ Piazza Santa Maria in Trastevere 6 ☎ 06 581 7145 🕐 Daily 10–10

PIAZZA SAN COSIMATO

It is a great shame that very few visitors manage to discover what this excellent mid-size general food market in Trastevere has to offer.

➕ E8 ✉ Piazza San Cosimato 🕐 Mon–Sat 7am–1pm

PORTA PORTESE

Everything and anything is for sale at this famous flea market, though the few genuine antiques are highly priced. By mid-morning crowds are huge, so come early and guard your belongings.

➕ F8 ✉ Via Porta Portese-Via Ippolito Nuevo 🕐 Sun 6.30am–2pm

LA RENELLA

Wonderful freshly baked bread and pizza all day, every day. This also means it is crowded at all hours. Try freshly baked, thick, unctuous slices of simple pizza *bianca*, topped with olive oil and rosemary, or opt for a number of different fresh toppings. Excellent cakes as well.

➕ E7 ✉ Via del Moro 15–16 ☎ 06 581 7265 🕐 Daily 7am–10pm

Entertainment and Nightlife

AKAB-CAVE
www.akabcove.it

In the lively Testaccio area, this very popular and long-established club is on two levels (one underground—hence Cave) with a garden area and varied music policy. International DJs and live rock bands.

🚇 Off map at G9 ⊠ Via Monte Testaccio 68–69 ☎ 06 578 2390 ⏱ Tue–Sat 11pm–4.30am 🚈 Piramide 🚌 23, 44, 170, 280 to Piazza di Porta San Paolo or Via Monte Testaccio 💵 Expensive

L'ALIBI
Primarily a gay disco, but not exclusively, L'Alibi is one of the most reliable (and most established) clubs now mushrooming in trendy Testaccio.

🚇 Off map at G9 ⊠ Via Monte Testaccio 40–44 ☎ 06 574 3448 ⏱ Wed–Sun 11pm–4.30am 🚈 Piramide 🚌 23, 44, 170, 280 to Piazza di Porta San Paolo or Via Monte Testaccio 💵 Expensive

BIG MAMA
www.bigmama.it

This is Rome's best blues club, which also hosts rock and jazz.

🚇 F8 ⊠ Vicolo San Francesco a Ripa 18 ☎ 06 581 2551 ⏱ Oct–end Jun, Tue–Sat 9pm–1.30am 🚌 H, 8, 780 to Viale di Trastevere 💵 Yearly membership (moderate) plus fee for concerts

CAFFÈ LATINO
Testaccio oldest club, devoted to eating, drinking,

live music and dance sessions. Mostly jazz, but rap, blues and other genres are here.

🚇 Off map at G9 ⊠ Via Monte Testaccio 96 ☎ 06 5728 8556 ⏱ Sep–end Jul, Tue–Thu, Sun 10.30pm–2.30am, Fri, Sat 10.30pm–4.30am 🚈 Piramide 🚌 3, 23, 30, 75, 280, 716 to Via Marmorata 💵 Membership (expensive)

ENOTECA TRASTEVERE
Tavern-like wine bar with more than 900 wines. During weekends, a pianist plays soft jazz and swing. Outdoor tables in summer.

🚇 F7 ⊠ Via della Lungaretta 86 ☎ 06 588 5659 ⏱ Daily 6pm–2am; closed Wed Dec–end Feb 🚌 H, 175 to Piazza Sidney Sonnino

LICENSING LAWS

Laws are much more liberal in Italy than in many countries. The legal age for buying alcoholic drink in bars or shops is 18, but it is very rare for proof of age to be demanded. Laws against drinking and driving, however, are firmly enforced. Opening times for premises licensed to sell alcohol are not set, and correspond to the individual opening times of each establishment. The only occasion on which restrictions on opening are set are before, during and after some football (soccer) matches.

PASQUINO
A Roman institution near Santa Maria in Trastevere, with three screens. Films are in their original language. Crowded espresso bar before screenings.

🚇 E7 ⊠ Piazza Sant'Egidio 10 ☎ 06 581 5208 ⏱ Daily; closed Jun–end Sep 🚈 Piramide 🚌 H, 23, 44, 56, 75, 280 to Viale Trastevere

RIPARTE CAFÉ
Popular modern and stylish nightspot; be sure to reserve ahead, particularly if you want to eat. Part of a four-star hotel.

🚇 F8 ⊠ Via Orti di Trastevere 7 ☎ 06 586 1816 ⏱ Mon–Sat 7.30am–12.30/1am 🚌 8, 780 💵 Expensive

LA SCALA
La Scala is one of the most popular bars and clubs in Trastevere. Loud, lively and young, it offers wine, beer, snacks and light meals and occasional live music. There are a few outside tables.

🚇 E7 ⊠ Via della Scala 4 ☎ 06 580 3763 ⏱ Daily noon–12.30am 🚌 H, 8, 780 to Piazza Sidney Sonnino or 23, 125, 280 to Lungarno Sanzio 💵 Free

TEATRO VASCELLO
On the edge of Trastevere, this is a small but good venue for experimental dance and some classic ballet.

🚇 D8 ⊠ Via Giacinto Carini 72 ☎ 06 588 1021 ⏱ Sep–end Jun, Tue–Sat 5.30–9, Sun 3–5 🚌 44, 75, 115, 710, 870

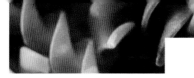

Restaurants

PRICES

Prices are approximate, based on a 3-course meal for one person.

€€€   over €50
€€   €30–€50
€   under €30

ALBERTO CIARLA (€€€)

This is among Rome's best fish restaurants, with a fine wine list. The food is elegantly presented, the candlelight lovely and the service impeccable.

🔢 E8 🖂 Piazza San Cosimato 40 ☎ 06 581 8668 or 06 581 6068 🕐 Dinner only Mon–Sat; closed 2 weeks in Aug and Jan 🚌 H, 8, 630, 780 to Viale di Trastevere

ALBERTO PICA (€)

Around 20 flavours of excellent quality ice cream; try the house specialties like green apple (*mele verde*) and Sicilian citrus (*agrumi di Sicilia*).

🔢 F6 🖂 Via della Seggiola 12, Cenci ☎ 06 686 8405 🕐 Mon–Sat 8am–1.30am (also Sun 4pm–2am Apr–end Oct); closed 2 weeks in Aug 🚌 8 to Via Arenula and 8, 46, 62, 63, 64, 70, 87, 186, 492 to Largo di Torre Argentina

AUGUSTO (€)

One of Trastevere's last remaining inexpensive and authentic family-run *trattorie*, with 50 places. No credit cards.

🔢 E7 🚌 10 🖂 Piazza de' Renzi 15 ☎ 06 580 3798 🕐 Daily 12–3.30, 8–11; closed Aug 🚌 23, 280 to Lungotevere Sanzio or H, 8, 780 to Piazza Sidney Sonnino

BIBLI (€€)

www.bibli.it

This Trastevere bookshop-cum-cafeteria is particularly popular for Sunday brunch. A selection of pastas, quiches, coucous with vegetable dishes are served buffet style.

🔢 F7 🖂 Via dei Fienaroli 28 ☎ 06 588 4097 🕐 Daily 11am–midnight; Mon 5.30–11.30 buffet-style dinner 🚌 H, 23, 44, 56, 75, 280 to Viale Trastevere or Piazza Sonnino

CHECCHINO DAL 1887 (€€€)

www.checchino-dal-1887.com

Robust appetites are required for the menu at this Testaccio establishment. Quintessential Roman dishes relying largely on offal are the

BUYING ICE CREAM

Ice cream (*gelato*) in a proper *gelateria* is sold either in a cone (*un cono*) or a paper cup (*una coppa*). Specify which you want and then decide how much you wish to pay: sizes of cone and cup go up in price bands, usually starting small and ending enormous. You can choose up to two or three flavours (more in bigger tubs) and will usually be asked if you want a swirl of cream (*panna*) to round things off.

specialty. Reservations advisable.

🔢 Off map G9 🖂 Via Monte Testaccio 30 ☎ 06 574 6318 🕐 Tue–Sat 12.30–3, 8–11; closed Aug 🚌 3, 60, 75, 118 to Piramide

DA MIRELLA (€)

Sells *granita*: crushed ice drenched in juice or syrup. The flavourings in this ice cream kiosk have been refined over many years; the ice is still ground by hand.

🔢 F7 🖂 Lungotevere Anguillara, Ponte Cestio 🕐 May–end Sep daily 8am–late 🚌 23, 280

DAR POETA (€)

A very popular and long-established little pizzeria hidden in a quiet street. The interior is simple but the pizza (and puddings) are excellent.

🔢 E7 🖂 Vicolo di Bologna 45 ☎ 06 588 0516 🕐 Daily dinner only 7.30–11 🚌 8, 870 and all services to Trastevere

DA VITTORIO (€)

Tiny Neapolitan-run Trastevere pizzeria that makes a good standby if Ivo (▷ 74) is busy.

🔢 E7 🖂 Via di San Cosimato 14a, off Piazza San Calisto ☎ 06 580 0353 🕐 Mon–Sat 7.30pm–midnight 🚌 H, 8, 780 to Viale di Trastevere

GIGGETTO (€)

A famous Romano-Jewish restaurant in the Ghetto district; almost as good and cheaper than Piperno (▷ 74).

🔛 G6 ✉ Via Portico
d'Ottavia 21a ☎ 06 686 1105
🕙 Tue– Sun 12.30–2.30,
7.30–10.30 🚌 H, 8, 63 to Via
Arenula and 46, 62, 63, 70
and other services to Largo di
Torre Argentina

IVO (€)
The best-known of
Trastevere's pizzerias.
Lines are common but
turnover is quick.
🔛 E7 ✉ Via di San
Francesco a Ripa 158 ☎ 06
581 7082 🕙 Wed–Mon
5.30–2am; closed 3 weeks in
Aug 🚌 H, 8, 780 to Viale
di Trastevere

PANATTONI (€)
Big, bright and often busy,
Panattoni is known locally
as 'L'Obitorio' (The
Morgue) on account of its
characteristic cold marble-
topped tables. Watch the
chef flip the pizzas at the
oven. Arrive early to get a
table outside.
🔛 F8 ✉ Viale di Trastevere
53 ☎ 06 580 0919
🕙 Thu–Tue 6.30pm–2am;
closed 3 weeks in Aug 🚌 H,
8, 780 to Viale di Trastevere

PARIS (€€)
An extremely popular and
elegant little restaurant
just south of Piazza Santa
Maria in Trastevere, and
known for its fish, pastas
and Roman cuisine.
Outside tables for alfresco
dining. Reserve ahead.
🔛 E7 ✉ Piazza San
Callisto 7a ☎ 06 581 5378
🕙 Tue–Sat 12.30–3, 8–11, Sun
12.30–3; closed 3 weeks in
Aug 🚌 H, 8, 780 to Piazza

Sidney Sonnino or 23, 280 to
Lungotevere Sanzio

PIPERNO (€€)
Much Roman cuisine is
based on the city's Jewish
culinary traditions. The
famous and resolutely traditional Piperno has been
a temple to Romano-
Jewish cuisine for over a
century. Reserve ahead.
🔛 F6 ✉ Via Monte de'
Cenci 9 ☎ 06 6880 6629/
2772 🕙 Tue–Sat 12.15–2.30,
8–10.30, Sun 12.15–3; closed
Aug 🚌 H, 8, 63 to Via Arenula
and 8, 46, 62, 63, 64, 70, 87,
492 to Largo di Torre Argentina

SABATINI (€€€)
Once Rome's most
famous restaurant,
Sabatini is still preferred
for its reliable food and
lovely setting, though

prices are higher than the
cooking deserves. Reserve
ahead.
🔛 E7 ✉ Piazza Santa Maria
in Trastevere 13 (and Vicolo
Santa Maria in Trastevere 18)
☎ 06 581 2026 or 06 581
8307) 🕙 Daily 12–2.30,
7.30–11; closed Aug 🚌 H, 8,
780 to Piazza Sidney Sonnino
or 23, 280 to Lungotevere
Sanzio

SACCHETTI (€)
Family-run bar in
Trastevere also good for
cakes and pastries.
🔛 E8 ✉ Piazza San
Cosimato 61–62 ☎ 06 581
5374 🕙 Tue–Sun 5am–11pm
🚌 H, 8, 780 to Viale
di Trastevere

SORA LELLA (€€)
Founded by the actress
Sora Lella, and now
presided over by her son
and nephews, this is a
two-room, wood-panelled
former *trattoria* on the
Isola Tiberina. Roman
cooking, with menu and
daily specials.
🔛 G7 ✉ Via Ponte Quattro
Capi 16 ☎ 06 686 1601
🕙 Mon–Sat 12.30–2.30,
7.30–10.30; closed Aug 🚌 23,
23, 63, 280 to Lungotevere
dei Cenci or Lungotevere
degli Anguillara

TRASTÈ (€)
Chic tea and coffee shop
serving light meals. Come
to chat, read the papers
and pass the time.
🔛 F7 ✉ Via della Lungaretta
76 ☎ 06 589 4430 🕙 Daily
5pm–2am 🚌 H, 8, 780 to
Piazza Sidney Sonnino

Northern Rome is a wonderful medley of open spaces, notably the Villa Borghese, historical and cultural attractions such as the Fontana di Trevi and the Spanish Steps, and Rome's finest shopping streets.

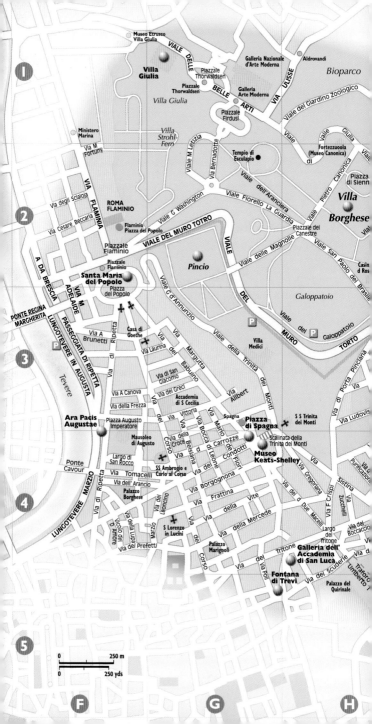

I

Museo Etrusco
Villa Giulia

VIALE DELLE

**Villa
Giulia**

Piazzale
Thorwaldsen

Galleria Nazionale
d'Arte Moderna

Aldrovandi

Bioparco

Piazzale
Thorwaldsen

Galleria
Arte Moderna

BELLE

Via ULISSE

Villa Giulia

ARTI

Viale del Giardino Zoologico

Piazzale
Firdusi

Ministero
Marina

Via M
Fortuny

*Villa
Strohl-
Fero*

Via Bernadotte

Viale

Via

giulia

Fortezzuola
(Museo Canonica)

Via Pietro Canonica

Tempio di
Esculapio

Piazza
di Sienn

2

VIA
FLAMINIA

Via degli Scialoia

Via Cesare Beccaria

ROMA
FLAMINIO

Viale G Washington

Viale dell'Aranciera

Viale Fiorello La Guardia

**Villa
Borghese**

A DA BRESCIA

Flaminio
Piazza del Popolo

VIALE DEL MURO TOTRO

VIALE

Piazzale dei
Canestre

Viale san Paolo del Brasile

Via

Casin
d Ros

Piazzale
Flaminio

VIA M ADELAIDE

Piazzale
Flaminio

**Santa Maria
del Popolo**

Piazza
del Popolo

Pincio

Viale delle Magnolie

Galopatoio

DEL

Casin
d Ros

PONTE REGINA
MARGHERITA

PASSEGGIATA DI RIPETTA

LUNGOTEVERE IN AUGUSTA

Via A
Brunetti

Casa di
Goethe

Via Ripetta

Viale G d'Annunzio

Viale della Trinità dei Monti

Viale

del

Viale del

Galopatoio

MURO

TORTO

3

Tevere

Via A Canova

Via della Frezza

Via Laurina

Via del Babuino

Via Margutta

Via di San
Giacomo

Via dei Greci

Accademia
di S Cecilia

Villa
Medici

Via di Porta Pinciana

Via

Via Ludovisi

**Ara Pacis
Augustae**

Piazza Augusto
Imperatore

Via Vittoria

Via Mario
de Fiori

Via della Croce

Via della
Croce

CVia della
Carrozze

Via Bocca di Leone

Via Belsiana

Via Alibert

Spagna

**Piazza
di Spagna**

S S Trinità
dei Monti

4

Mausoleo
di Augusto

Largo di
San Rocco

SS Ambrogio e
Carlo al Corso

Via Tomacelli

Via dell'Arancio

Palazzo
Borghese

Via Condotti

Via Borgognona

Via del Corso

Via del Leoncino

Frattina

Scalinata della
Trinità dei Monti

**Museo
Keats-Shelley**

Via Gregoriana

Via Sistina

Via del d Due Macelli

Via F Crispi

Via Zucchelli

Vite

PONTE
MARZIO

LUNGOTEVERE MARZIO

Via di Ripetta

Vicolo del
D'Amore

Via della Lupa

Via dei Prefetti

Via del
Leoncino

S Lorenzo
in Lucini

Via

della

Via della Mercede

Palazzo
Marignoli

del

Via del Corso

Tritone

Via del d Scuderie

Via del Tritone

Largo
del
Tritone

Via del Boccaccio

Via

**Galleria dell'
Accademia
di San Luca**

Traforo
Umberto I

5

**Fontana
di Trevi**

Palazzo del
Quirinale

0 ———— 250 m

0 ———— 250 yds

F   **G**   **H**

Museo e
Galleria Borghese

Viale del t zoologico

Viale dei Daini

Via d Due Mascheroni

Viale

dell'

Uccelliera

Pupazzi

Piazzale
dei Cavalli
Marini

dei Cavalli

Viale del Museo Marini

Via Isonzo

VIA PINCIANA

Via Po

Borghese

VIA PINCIANA

CORSO D'ITALIA

CAMPANIA

VIA

Sardegna

Via Romagna

VIA LUCANIA

VIA SICILIA

VIA CALABRIA

Via Puglie

Via Sicilia

Via Nervia

Via Collina

VIA VITTORIO VENETO

Lombardia

Via Marche

Abruzzi

BONCOMPAGNI

Piemonte

Via Luculio

Sallustiana

Via Quintino Sella

Flavia

XX SETTEMBRE

Emilia

Via Liguria

VIA L BISSOLATI

Via Umbria

Via G Carducci

Aureliana

Via Antonio Salandra

VIA

Vittorio Veneto

Santa Maria
della Vittoria

CERNAIA

Via Volturno

Santa Maria della
Concezione

Salita di Tolentino

Via S Nd a Tolentino

S Barberini

Via Parigi

Barberini
Fontana Trevi

Via di S N da S Tolentino

SETTEMBRE

Terme di
Diocleziano

Fontana
del Tritone

Piazza
Barberini

Palazzo
Barberini

XX

VIA

Via Firenze

VIA V E ORLANDO

Repubblica
Teatro Opera

Via Torino

S Maria
d Angeli

Fontana
delle Naiadi

VIALE L EINAUDI

VIALE ENRICO DE NICOLA

Via delle Quattro Fontane

Piazza della
Repubblica

Giardini

Via Modena

VIA NAZIONALE

Palazzo Massimo
alle Terme

Giardini del
Quirinale

San Carlo alle
Quattro Fontane

Teatro dell'
Opera

VIA G AMENDOLA

VIA DEL QUIRINALE

Sant'Andrea
al Quirinale

VIA

Via di San Viale

Via Napoli

Via del Viminale

VIA TORINO

Termini

Placenza

Via Genova

AGOSTINO DEPRETIS

Via d'Azeglio

Via Principe Amedeo

Via Manin

Via Milano

VIA

Palermo

Piazza del
Viminale

VIA CAVOUR

Via Daniele

J   K

Fontana di Trevi

TOP
25

Remember to toss a coin in the fountain (left). The Trevi in all its floodlit glory (right)

THE BASICS

🕂 G5
✉ Piazza Fontana di Trevi
🕐 Always open
🚇 Spagna or Barberini
🚌 C3, 52, 53, 61, 62, 71, 95, 117, 119 and other routes to Via del Corso and Via del Tritone
♿ Access via cobbled street
🎟 Free

HIGHLIGHTS

- *Oceanus* (Neptune)
- *Allegory of Health* (right of *Oceanus*)
- *Virgin Indicating the Spring to Soldiers*
- *Allegory of Abundance* (left of *Oceanus*)
- *Agrippa Approving the Design of the Aqueduct*
- *Triton with Horse* (on the right, symbolizing the ocean in repose)
- *Triton with Horse* (on the left, symbolizing a tempestuous sea)
- Façade of Santi Vincenzo e Anastasio
- Baroque interior of Santa Maria in Trivio

There is no lovelier surprise than that which confronts you as you emerge from the tight warren of streets around the Fontana di Trevi, the city's most famous fountain—a sight 'silvery to the eye and ear', in the words of Charles Dickens.

Virgin discovery In its earliest guise the Fontana di Trevi lay at the end of the Aqua Virgo, or Acqua Vergine, an aqueduct built by Agrippa in 19BC (supposedly filled with Rome's sweetest waters). The spring that fed it was reputedly discovered by a virgin, hence its name. (She is said to have shown her discovery to some Roman soldiers, a scene—along with Agrippa's approval of the aqueduct's plans—described in bas-reliefs on the fountain's second tier.) The fountain's liveliness and charm is embodied in the pose of *Oceanus*, the central figure, and the two giant tritons and their horses (symbolizing a calm and a stormy sea) drawing his chariot. Other statues represent Abundance and Health and, above, the Four Seasons, which each carry gifts.

The fountains A new fountain was built in 1453, ordered by Pope Nicholas V who paid for it by taxing wine. Its name came from the three roads (*tre vie*) that converged on the piazza. The present fountain was commissioned by Pope Clement XII in 1732 and finished in 1762: Its design was inspired by the Arch of Constantine and is attributed to Nicola Salvi, with possible contributions from Bernini. Those wishing to return to Rome toss a coin (over the shoulder) into the fountain.

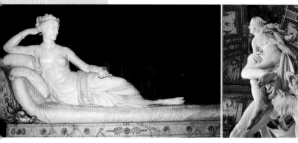

Canova's Paolina Borghese *(left)* and Bernini's Rape of Proserpine *(right)*

Museo e Galleria Borghese

The Galleria Borghese may be small, but what it lacks in quantity it makes up for in quality. It combines paintings and sculptures, including many masterpieces by Gian Lorenzo Bernini, Raphael, Caravaggio and others.

Seductress The Villa Borghese was designed in 1613 as a summer retreat for Cardinal Scipione Borghese, nephew of Pope Paul V, who accumulated most of the collection (acquired by the state in 1902). Scipione was an enthusiastic patron of Bernini, whose works dominate the gallery. The museum's foremost masterpiece is Antonio Canova's *Paolina Borghese* (1804), Napoleon's sister and wife of Camillo Borghese. Depicted bare-breasted, with a come-hither hauteur, Paolina was just as seductive in life. Her jewels, clothes, lovers and the servants she used as footstools all excited gossip.

Bernini His *David* (1623–24) is said to be a self-portrait, while *Apollo and Daphne* (1622–25), in the next room, is considered his masterpiece. Other Bernini works include the *Rape of Proserpine* (1622) and *Truth Unveiled by Time* (1652).

The paintings Foremost in this wonderful collection are works by Raphael (*The Deposition of Christ*, 1507), Titian (*Sacred and Profane Love*, 1512), Caravaggio (*Boy with a Fruit Basket* and *Madonna dei Palafrenieri*, 1605) and Correggio (*Danae*, 1530).

THE BASICS

www.galleriaborghese.it
+ J2
⊠ Piazzale Scipione Borghese 5
☎ 06 841 7645; obligatory reservations 06 328 101; www.ticketeria.it
🕐 Tue–Sun 9–7. Closed public holidays
🚇 Spagna or Flaminio
🚌 116 to Viale del Museo Borghese, or 52, 53, 910 to Via Pinciana or C3, 19 to Via delle Belle Arti
♿ Steps to front entrance
💷 Expensive

HIGHLIGHTS

● *Paolina Borghese*, Canova
● *David*, Bernini
● *Apollo and Daphne*, Bernini
● *Madonna dei Palafrenieri*, Caravaggio
● *Sacred and Profane Love*, Titian
● *Deposition of Christ*, Raphael

Palazzo Barberini

TOP 25

Frescoes outlined in gold adorn the palazzo (left). Raphael's La Fornarina (right)

THE BASICS

✚ J4

✉ Via Barberini 18

☎ 06 482 4184; online booking www.ticketeria.it

🕐 Tue–Sun 9–7

Ⓜ Barberini

🚍 52, 53, 61, 62, 63, 71, 80, 95, 116, 119 to Via del Tritone or H, 40, 60, 64, 70, 71, 116T, 170 to Via Nazionale

♿ Few

💷 Moderate

HIGHLIGHTS

● Elicoidale
● *Madonna and Child* and *Annunciation*, Filippo Lippi
● *Holy Family* and *Madonna and Saints*, Andrea del Sarto
● *Madonna and Child*, Beccafumi
● *La Fornarina*, Raphael
● *Adoration of the Shepherds* and *Baptism of Christ*, El Greco
● *Judith and Holofernes* and *Narciso*, Caravaggio
● *Beatrice Cenci*, attributed to Guido Reni
● *Henry VIII*, attributed to Holbein
● *The Triumph of Divine Providence*, Pietro da Cortona (Gran Salone)

The magnificent Palazzo Barberini— designed by Bernini, Borromini and Carlo Maderno—houses a stupendous ceiling fresco and one of Rome's finest art collections, the Galleria Nazionale d'Arte Antica.

Urban's grandeur The palace was commissioned by Maffeo Barberini for his family when he became Pope Urban VIII in 1623. It was begun by Carlo Maderno and completed by Bernini. The epitome of Rome's high baroque style, it is a maze of suites, apartments and staircases, many still swathed in their sumptuous original decoration. Overshadowing all is the Gran Salone, dominated by Pietro da Cortona's rich ceiling frescos, glorifying Urban as an agent of Divine Providence. The central windows and oval spiral staircase (Scala Elicoidale) are the work of Borromini.

The collection *'Antica'* here means old rather than ancient. Probably the most popular painting in the collection is Raphael's *La Fornarina* (also attributed to Giulio Romano). It is reputedly a portrait of one of the artist's several mistresses, identified later as the daughter of a *fornaio* (baker). It was executed in the year of the painter's death, a demise brought on, it is said, by his mistress's unrelenting passion. Elsewhere, eminent Italian works from Filippo Lippi, Andrea del Sarto, Caravaggio and Guido Reni stand alongside paintings by leading foreign artists. Also here is a rich collection of paintings, furniture, ceramics and other beautiful decorative arts.

This popular meeting place (left and right) is used as a stage for fashion shows (middle)

Piazza di Spagna

Neither old nor particularly striking, the Spanish Steps are nonetheless one of Rome's most popular meeting points, thanks largely to their views, at the heart of Piazza di Spagna in the city's exclusive shopping district.

Spanish Steps Despite their name, the Spanish Steps were commissioned by the French ambassador, Étienne Gueffier, who in 1723 sought to link Piazza di Spagna with the French-owned church of Trinità dei Monti on the hill above. A century earlier the piazza had housed the headquarters of the Spanish ambassador to the Holy See, hence the name of the steps and the square.

Around the steps At the base of the steps is the Fontana della Barcaccia, commissioned in 1627 by Urban VIII and designed either by Gian Lorenzo Bernini or by his less famous father, Pietro. The eccentric design represents a half-sunken boat. As you face the steps from below, to your right stands the Museo Keats–Shelley, a fascinating collection of literary memorabilia and a working library housed in the lodgings where the poet John Keats died in 1821. At the top of the steps you can enjoy views past Palazzo Barberini (▷ 80) and towards the Quirinal Hill; walk into the simple Trinità dei Monti, with its outside double stairs by Domenico Fontana; and visit the beautiful gardens of the 16th-century Villa Medici, the seat of the French Academy in Rome, where scholars study painting, sculpture, architecture, engraving and music.

THE BASICS

🔒 G4
✉ Piazza di Spagna
☎ Caffè Greco 06 679 1700. Villa Medici 06 679 8381
🕐 Spanish Steps always open. Trinità dei Monti daily 10–12.30, 4–6. Villa Medici occasionally open for exhibitions.
🍴 Babington's Tea Rooms (▷ 90)
Ⓜ Spagna
🚌 119 to Piazza di Spagna
♿ None for the Spanish Steps
🎟 Free

HIGHLIGHTS

● Spanish Steps
● Museo Keats–Shelley (▷ 87)
● Trinità dei Monti
● Fontana della Barcaccia
● Babington's Tea Rooms (▷ 90)
● Villa Medici gardens
● Pincio Gardens (▷ 87)

Palazzo Massimo alle Terme

TOP 25

HIGHLIGHTS

● *Niobid from the Hortus Sallustiani* (Room VIII)
● *The Lancellotti Discobolus* (Room VI)
● *The Sleeping Hermaphrodite* (Room VII)
● House of Livia (Room II)
● *The Villa Farnesina* (Gallery II, Rooms III–V)

TIP

● The combined ticket is valid for all parts of the Museo Nazionale Romano, notably the Palazzo Altemps.

A sublime collection of Greek and Roman sculpture with outstanding and unique displays of ancient Roman wall paintings and mosaics dating from end of the Republican age to the late Imperial age.

The building The Palazzo Massimo is an elegant and airy 19th-century palace, beautifully renovated for the millennium. The palace, designed by Camillo Pistrucci, was built in the late 19th century by the Massimo family to replace an earlier one demolished to make way for the Termini station. In 1981 the palace was acquired by the state, and in the 1990s it was transformed into one of Rome's most attractive museums. The palace has four floors of museum space, a modern library, a conference room and a computer-based documentation area.

Lovingly restored, the Palazzo Massimo was a Jesuit college until 1960 (left) but now houses outstanding displays of ancient Roman wall paintings and mosaics (right)

The collection One of the two buildings (the other being Palazzo Altemps, ▷ 42–43) housing Rome's magnificent Classical collections, here you'll find some of Rome's greatest Classical treasures, ranging from naked gods and games players to sarcophagi and goddesses. Don't miss the superb portrait busts or the wonderful Roman frescos and mosaics on the upper floor.

Lancellotti Discobolus This fine marble copy of the great *Discus Thrower* dates from the mid-second century AD, and is one of the most famous copies of the 5th-century BC works. Discovered in the 18th century, it was sent to Germany during World War II and returned in 1948. It reproduces an original bronze, showing an athlete throwing a discus—probably the work of Myron, a Greek sculptor renowned for his portraits of athletes.

THE BASICS

www.pierreci.it
+ K4–5
✉ Piazza dei Cinquecento 67–Largo di Villa Peretti 1
☎ Reservations 06 3996 7700
🕐 Tue–Sun 9–7.45
Ⓜ Repubblica
🚌 All services to Termini and Piazza dei Cinquecento
💰 Expensive (joint pass available with Palazzo Altemps, Crypta Balbi and Terme di Diocleziano)

Santa Maria del Popolo

Carracci's Assumption of the Virgin *(left). Inside is a wealth of artistic works (right)*

THE BASICS

- ✚ F2
- ✉ Piazza del Popolo 12
- ☎ 06 361 0836
- 🕐 Mon–Sat 8–1.30, 4.30–7.30, Sun 8am–7.30pm
- 🚇 Flaminio
- 🚌 117, 119 to Piazza del Popolo
- ♿ Few
- 🎟 Free

HIGHLIGHTS

- Cappella Chigi
- *Conversion of St. Paul* and *Crucifixion of St. Peter*, Caravaggio
- *Coronation of the Virgin*, Pinturicchio
- Tombs of Ascanio Sforza and Girolamo Basso della Rovere
- *Nativity*, Pinturicchio
- Fresco: *Life of San Girolamo*, Tiberio d'Assisi
- *Delphic Sybil*, Pinturicchio
- Altar, Andrea Bregno
- Stained glass
- *Assumption of the Virgin*, Annibale Carracci

Santa Maria del Popolo's appeal stems from its intimate size and location, and from a wonderfully varied and rich collection of works of art ranging from masterpieces by Caravaggio to some of Rome's earliest stained-glass windows.

Renaissance achievement Founded in 1099 on the site of Nero's grave, Santa Maria del Popolo was rebuilt by Pope Sixtus IV in 1472 and extended later by Bramante and Bernini. The right nave's first chapel, the Cappella della Rovere, is decorated with frescos—*Life of San Girolamo* (1485–90)—by Tiberio d'Assisi, a pupil of Pinturicchio whose *Nativity* (*c*1490) graces the chapel's main altar. The apse contains two fine stained-glass windows (1509) by the French artist Guillaume de Marcillat. On either side are the greatest of the church's monuments: the tombs of the cardinals Ascanio Sforza (1505, left) and Girolamo Basso della Rovere (1507, right). Both are the work of Andrea Sansovino. High on the walls are superb and elegant frescos (1508–10) of the Virgin, Evangelists, the Fathers of the Church and Sybils by Pinturicchio.

North nave The first chapel of the left transept, the Cappella Cerasi, contains three major paintings: the altarpiece, *Assumption of the Virgin*, by Annibale Carracci; and Caravaggio's dramatic *Conversion of St. Paul* and the *Crucifixion of St. Peter* (all 1601). The famous Cappella Chigi (1513), the second chapel in the north aisle, was commissioned by the Sienese banker Agostino Chigi.

Villa Giulia, built to a design by Giacomo da Vignola, displays beautiful frescos

Villa Giulia

NORTHERN ROME

TOP 25

The Museo Nazionale Etrusca di Villa Giulia houses the world's greatest collection of Etruscan art and objects. The exhibits are not always perfectly presented, but it is a revelation to discover this mysterious civilization.

The villa Built in 1550–55 as a country house and garden for the hedonistic Pope Julius III, the Villa Giulia was designed by some of the leading architects of the day, including Michelangelo and Georgio Vasari.

The collection The exhibits are generally divided between finds from Etruscan sites in northern Etruria (western central Italy) and from excavations in the south (Nemi and Praeneste), including objects made by the Greeks. Most notable are the Castellani exhibits, which include vases, cups and ewers, and jewellery from the Minoan period (the latter collection is one of the villa's special treasures). To see the most striking works of art, be selective. Pick through the numerous vases noting the *Tomba del Guerriero* and the *Cratere a Volute*. Note also the *Sarcofago degli Sposi*, a 6th-century BC sarcophagus with figures of a married couple reclining together on a banqueting couch; the engraved marriage coffer known as the *Cista Ficoroni* (4th century BC); the giant terra-cotta figures, *Hercules and Apollo*; the temple sculptures from Falerii Veteres; and the valuable 7th-century BC relics in gold, silver, bronze and ivory from the Barberini and Bernardini tombs in Praeneste, 39km (24 miles) east of Rome.

THE BASICS

🔲 G1

✉ Piazzale di Villa Giulia 9

☎ 06 322 6571; reservations 06 824 620 online booking, www.ticketeria.it

🕐 Tue–Sun 8.30am–7.30pm

🍴 Café and shop

🚇 Flaminio

🚌 3 or 19 to Viale delle Belle Arti

♿ Good

💰 Moderate

HIGHLIGHTS

● *Lamine d'Oro*, Sala di Pyrgi: a gold tablet
● Vase: *Tomba del Guerriero*
● Terra-cottas: *Hercules and Apollo*
● Sarcofago degli Sposi
● Castellani Collection
● Vase: *Cratere a Volute*
● Finds from Falerii Veteres
● Tomb relics: Barberini and Bernardini
● Marriage coffer: *Cista Ficoroni*
● Gardens with Nymphaeum and reconstructed 'Temple of Alatri'

More to See

★

ARA PACIS AUGUSTAE
www.arapacis.it
The Altar of Peace, now contained within architect Richard Meier's controversial glass pavilion (opened in 2006) is decorated with bas-reliefs from 9BC. It was built to celebrate Augustus's triumphal return to Rome after campaigns in Spain and Gaul, and to commemorate the peace he had established throughout the Roman world. The outside of the enclosure is decorated with mythological scenes and grand processional friezes in which life-size figures portray Augustus, the imperial family, officials and other notables. The altar has recently reopened to the public within a new building.

⊞ F4 ✉ Lungotevere in Augusta ☎ 06 8205 9127 🕓 Tue–Sun 9–7 🚌 224, 913 to Piazza Augusto Imperatore or 224, 590, 628, 926 to Lungotevere in Augusta or 117, 119 to Via di Ripetta 💷 Moderate

FONTANA DEL TRITONE
Like its companion piece, the Fontana delle Api, the Fountain of Triton (1643) was also designed by Bernini for Urban VIII. One of the sculptor's earliest fountains, the Fontana del Tritone depicts four dolphins supporting twin scallop shells bearing the Barberini coat of arms, on which the triumphant Triton is enthroned.

⊞ H4 ✉ Piazza Barberini 🚇 Barberini 🚌 52, 53, 61, 62, 80, 95, 116, 119 to Piazza Barberini or Via del Tritone

GALLERIA DELL'ACCADEMIA DI SAN LUCA
www.accademiasanluca.it
This gallery was founded to promote the training of artists in Renaissance techniques. From 1633, every artist member of the academy had to donate a work of art, resulting in a wonderful collection that includes paintings by Raphael, Canova, Van Dyck, Rubens and Titian, to name a few.

⊞ H4 ✉ Piazza dell'Accademia di San Luca 77 ☎ 06 679 8850 🕓 Call for latest openings or visit website 🚌 52, 53, 60, 61, 62, 71, 80, 85, 160, 850 to Piazza San Silvestro 💷 Free

Ara Pacis Augustae, a memorial to the peace brought about by Augustus

A feature at the Galleria dell'Accademia di San Luca

MUSEO KEATS–SHELLEY

www.keats-shelley-house.org
Since 1909 this has been a museum
and library for students of the
Romantic poets Keats and Shelley.
Books, pictures and essays lie scat-
tered around the 18th-century house.
🔲 G4 ✉ Piazza di Spagna ☎ 06 678
4235 🕐 Mon–Fri 9–1, 3–6, Sat 11–2, 3–6
Ⓢ Spagna 🚌 119 to Piazza di Spagna
👋 Inexpensive

PINCIO

The park was laid out in the early 19th
century. Walk to the Pincio from Piazza
del Popolo or Piazza di Spagna to enjoy wonderful views (best at dusk)
across the rooftops to St. Peter's.
🔲 G2 ✉ Piazza del Pincio 🕐 Daily
dawn–dusk 🚌 95, 117, 119 to Piazzale
Flaminio or Piazza del Popolo 👋 Free

SANTA MARIA DELLA CONCEZIONE

Lying in the crypt of Santa Maria della
Concezione, built in 1624, are the
remains of 4,000 Capuchin monks,
some still dressed in jaunty clothes,
the bones of others crafted into
macabre chandeliers and bizarre wall
decorations. The bodies were originally buried in soil especially imported
from Jerusalem. When this ran out
they were left uncovered, a practice
that continued until 1870.
🔲 H4 ✉ Via Vittorio Veneto 27 ☎ 06 487
1185 🕐 Church daily 7–12, 3/4–7. Crypt
(Cimitero dei Cappuccini) Wed–Mon 9–12,
3–6 🚌 52, 53, 80, 95, 116, 119 and other
services to Via Vittorio Veneto 👋 Free
(donation to visit crypt)

VILLA BORGHESE

Rome's largest central park (▷ 88)
was laid out between 1613 and 1616
as the grounds of the Borghese family's summer villa. Redesigned in the
18th century, it still provides a shady
retreat. Walkways, woods and lakes
are complemented by fountains, a
racetrack and children's playgrounds.
There is also a zoo (Bioparco).
🔲 H2 ✉ Porta Pinciana-Via Flaminia
🕐 Daily dawn–dusk; Bioparco daily 9.30–5/6
Ⓢ Flaminio 🚌 3, 19, 88, 95, 116, 117, 119,
495 👋 Free; Bioparco expensive

The crypt, Santa Maria della Concezione

The Temple of Esculapio, at the Villa
Borghese

Villa Borghese

A stroll in this park, once the estate of Cardinal Scipione Borghese, is the perfect antidote to the turmoil of Rome's busy streets.

DISTANCE: 2km (1.2 miles) **ALLOW:** 2 hours

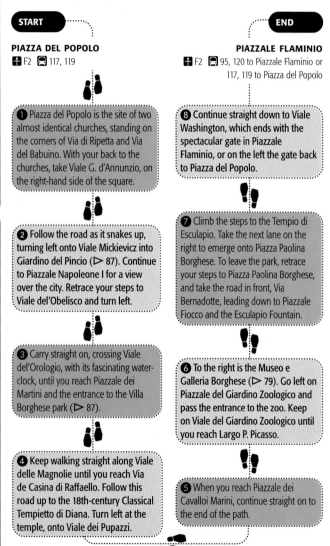

START

PIAZZA DEL POPOLO
🚇 F2 🚌 117, 119

END

PIAZZALE FLAMINIO
🚇 F2 🚌 95, 120 to Piazzale Flaminio or 117, 119 to Piazza del Popolo

1 Piazza del Popolo is the site of two almost identical churches, standing on the corners of Via di Ripetta and Via del Babuino. With your back to the churches, take Viale G. d'Annunzio, on the right-hand side of the square.

2 Follow the road as it snakes up, turning left onto Viale Mickievicz into Giardino del Pincio (▷ 87). Continue to Piazzale Napoleone I for a view over the city. Retrace your steps to Viale del'Obelisco and turn left.

3 Carry straight on, crossing Viale del'Orologio, with its fascinating water-clock, until you reach Piazzale dei Martini and the entrance to the Villa Borghese park (▷ 87).

4 Keep walking straight along Viale delle Magnolie until you reach Via de Casina di Raffaello. Follow this road up to the 18th-century Classical Tempietto di Diana. Turn left at the temple, onto Viale dei Pupazzi.

8 Continue straight down to Viale Washington, which ends with the spectacular gate in Piazzale Flaminio, or on the left the gate back to Piazza del Popolo.

7 Climb the steps to the Tempio di Esculapio. Take the next lane on the right to emerge onto Piazza Paolina Borghese. To leave the park, retrace your steps to Piazza Paolina Borghese, and take the road in front, Via Bernadotte, leading down to Piazzale Fiocco and the Esculapio Fountain.

6 To the right is the Museo e Galleria Borghese (▷ 79). Go left on Piazzale del Giardino Zoologico and pass the entrance to the zoo. Keep on Viale del Giardino Zoologico until you reach Largo P. Picasso.

5 When you reach Piazzale dei Cavalloi Marini, continue straight on to the end of the path.

Shopping

ANTICA ENOTECA
An old-fashioned shop where you can purchase wine by the bottle or by the glass amid trickling fountains.
➕ G3 ✉ Via della Croce 76b ☎ 06 679 0896 ⏰ Daily 11.30am–midnight

AVC DI ADRIANA CAMPANILE
Bright, modern and wearable styles for women with the distinctive red heart logo of Adriana Campanile.
➕ G3 ✉ Piazza di Spagna 88 ☎ 06 6992 2355 ⏰ Mon–Sat 10.30–7.30, Sun 11–1, 2–7.30

BATTISTONI
Traditional tailor's shop in business for over half a century.
➕ G4 ✉ Via Condotti 61a ☎ 06 697 6111 ⏰ Tue–Sat 10–7, Mon 3–7.30

ERMENEGILDO ZEGNA
Informal suits and jackets in exquisite, expensive fabrics. Also stocks shirts, sweaters and accessories.
➕ G4 ✉ Via Borgognona 7e ☎ 06 678 9143 ⏰ Mon–Sat 10–7.30, Sun 3.30–7.30

FAUSTO SANTINI
An iconoclast who designs witty, innovative and bizarre shoes.
➕ G4 ✉ Via Frattina 120–1 ☎ 06 678 4114 ⏰ Mon–Sat 10–7.30, Sun 12–7.30

FERRAGAMO
An established family firm; probably Italy's most renowned shoe shop.
➕ G4 ✉ Via Condotti 73–4 (women's) ☎ 06 679 1565; ✉ Via Condotti 65 (men's) ☎ 06 678 1130 ⏰ Mon–Sat 10–7, last Sun of month 12–7

GINORI
One of the top Italian names in modern and traditional glass and china.
➕ G3 ✉ Piazza Trinita dei Monti 18b ☎ 06 679 3836 ⏰ Tue–Sat 10–7.30

GIORGIO ARMANI
King of cut and classic, understated elegance.
➕ G4 ✉ Via Condotti 77 ☎ 06 699 1460 ⏰ Mon–Sat 10–7

GUCCI
Expensive and high-quality bags, shoes and leather goods are a feature of this famous name.
➕ G3 ✉ Via Condotti 8 ☎ 06 679 0405 ⏰ Mon–Sat 10–7, Sun 2.30–7

MARELLA
The showcase shop for the Marella label offers classic, well-made designs at reasonable prices.
➕ G4 ✉ Via Frattina 129–31 ☎ 06 6992 3800 ⏰ Tue–Sat 10–7.30, Mon, Sun 11–2, 3–7

LA PERLA
Italian lingerie is among the best in the world, and this reputation is more than upheld by La Perla.
➕ G4 ✉ Via Condotti 79 ☎ 06 6994 1934 ⏰ Tue–Sat 10–7, Mon 3–7

PINEIDER
Rome's most expensive and exclusive stationers. Virtually any design can be printed onto personalized visiting cards.
➕ H4 ✉ Via dei Due Macelli 68 ☎ 06 678 9013 ⏰ Mon–Sat 10–7, Sun 10–2, 3–7

PRADA
The Rome flagship store of the celebrated Milan-based designer.
➕ G4 ✉ Via Condotti 92–5 ☎ 06 679 0897 ⏰ Daily 10–7

SERGIO DI CORI
Romans who need gloves look no further than this tiny shop.
➕ G3 ✉ Piazza di Spagna 53 ☎ 06 678 4439 ⏰ Mon–Sat 9.30–7.30, Sun 11–7

SALES AND BARGAINS
Sales (*saldi*) in Rome are not always the bargains they seem. That said, many shoe shops and top designers cut their prices drastically during summer and winter sales (mid-Jul to mid-Sep and Jan to mid-Mar). Other lures to get you into a shop, notably the offer of *sconti* (discounts) and *vendite promozionali* (promotional offers), rarely save you any money. It can occasionally be worth asking for a discount (*uno sconto*), particularly if you are paying cash for an expensive item, or buying several items from one shop.

Entertainment and Nightlife

GILDA

The louche and languid atmosphere at this club has been attracting stars and VIPs for years. Smart jacket required.

🔢 G4 ✉ Via Mario de' Fiori 97 ☎ 06 678 4838 🕙 Thu–Sun 11pm–4am 🚇 Spagna 🚌 52, 53, 61, 71, 85, 160, 850 to Piazza San Silvestro 💷 Expensive

GREGORY'S

www.gregorysjazzclub.it
Relaxed club, and one of the few places in central Rome where you can listen to jazz.

🔢 H4 ✉ Via Gregoriana

54/a ☎ 06 679 6386 🕙 Tue–Sun 8pm–2/3.30am 🚌 119 to Piazza di Spagna 💷 Variable

TEATRO DELL'OPERA DI ROMA

www.opera.roma.it
One of Italy's top opera houses; also an official venue for the ballet.

🔢 J–K5 ✉ Piazza Beniamo Gigli 8 ☎ 06 481 7003; box office 06 481 601 🚇 Termini 🚌 H, 40, 60, 64, 70, 71, 170 to Via Nazionale or services o Termini

TEATRO OLIMPICO

This is where the

Filarmonica di Rome performs, as well as other international dance and music ensembles.

🔢 Off map at F1 ✉ Piazza Gentile da Fabriano ☎ 06 323 4890 Box Office 06 326 5991 🚌 225 Piazza Mancini

ZEST

The sleek, modern bar of the ES Hotel. Sip drinks in the stylish minimalist interior, or in summer outside on the terrace.

🔢 L5 ✉ ES Hotel, Via Filippo Turati 171 ☎ 06 444 841 🕙 Daily 10am–1.30pm 🚇 Vittorio Emanuele 🚌 70, 71 💷 Free

Restaurants

PRICES

Prices are approximate, based on a 3-course meal for one person.

€€€	over €50
€€	€30–€50
€	under €30

BABINGTON'S TEA ROOMS (€€€)

Mix with the well-heeled at Babington's, set up by a pair of English spinsters in 1896. Prices are sky-high, but the tea is the best in Rome.

🔢 G3 ✉ Piazza di Spagna 23 ☎ 06 678 6027 🕙 Daily 9am–8.15pm 🚇 Spagna 🚌 119 to Piazza di Spagna

EST! EST! EST! (€)

Among Rome's oldest and best pizzerias.

🔢 J5 ✉ Via Genova 32 ☎ 06 488 1107 🕙 Tue–Sun 6.30–11.30pm; closed Aug 🚇 Repubblica 🚌 H, 40, 60, 64, 70, 117, 170 to Via Nazionale

RESTAURANT ETIQUETTE

Italians have a strong sense of how to behave, which applies in restaurants as much as anywhere It is considered bad form to order only one course in more sophisticated restaurants–if that is what you want, go to a pizzeria or *trattoria*.

LEONCINO (€)

Little has changed at this wonderful old-fashioned pizzeria for over 30 years.

🔢 G4 ✉ Via del Leoncino 28, Piazza San Lorenzo in Lucina ☎ 06 687 6306 🕙 Mon–Tue, Thu–Fri 1–2.30pm, 7pm– midnight, Sat 7pm–midnight 🚇 Spagna 🚌 81, 119 to Via del Corso-Via Tomacelli

PIZZA CIRO (€)

The pizzas and pasta here are far better than the lurid wall murals.

🔢 G4 ✉ Via della Mercede 43 ☎ 06 678 6015 🕙 Daily noon–1/2am 🚇 Spagna 🚌 All services to Via del Corso and Via del Tridente

Vatican City is a separate sovereign state within Rome, and home to the great basilica of St. Peter's and a series of museums with some of the world's richest and most varied collections of art and objects.

Around the Vatican

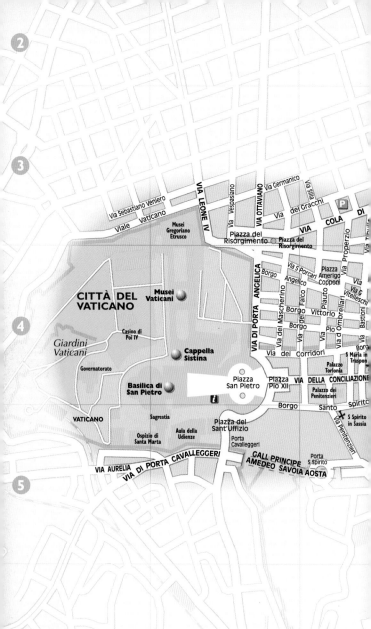

CITTÀ DEL VATICANO

Musei Vaticani

Giardini Vaticani

Casino di Poi IV

Governatorato

Cappella Sistina

Basilica di San Pietro

VATICANO

Sagrestia

Ospizio di Santa Marta

Aula della Udienze

Piazza San Pietro

Piazza Pio XII

Piazza del Sant'Uffizio

Porta Cavalleggeri

VIA AURELIA

VIA DI PORTA CAVALLEGGERI

Via Sebastiano Veniero

Viale Vaticano

Musei Gregoriano Etrusco

VIA LEONE IV

Via Vespasiano

VIA OTTAVIANO

Via Germanico

Via del Gracchi

Via Sila

VIA COLA DI

Piazza del Risorgimento

Piazza del Risorgimento

Via Properzio

Borgo

VIA ANGELICA

VIA DI PORTA ANGELICA

Via S Porcari

Borgo Angelico

Via del Mascherino

Borgo Falco

Borgo Vittorio

Borgo Pio

Via Plauto

Via Pio O'Ombrellari

Via dei Corridori

Piazza Amerigo Capponi

Via G Vitelleschi

Via Bastion

S Maria in Traspon

Borgo

Palazzo Torlonia

Palazzo dei Penitenzieri

VIA DELLA CONCILIAZIONE

Borgo

Santo

Spirito

S Spirito in Sassia

Via Penitenzieri

GALL PRINCIPE AMEDEO SAVOIA AOSTA

Porta S.Spirito

0   250 m

0   250 yds

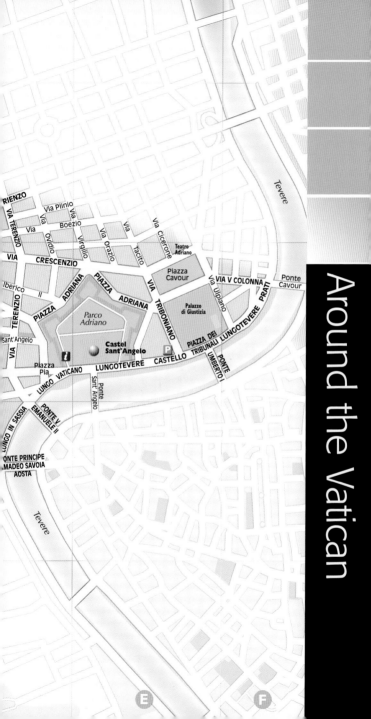

Basilica di San Pietro

The famous dome of St. Peter's viewed from the inside (right) and out (left)

THE BASICS

+ B–C4

✉ Piazza San Pietro, Città del Vaticano

☎ 06 6988 1662/3462

🕐 Mid-Mar–end Sep daily 7–7 (Oct–end Feb until 6). Dome Apr–end Sep 8am–5.45; Oct–end Mar 8am–4.45. Grottos Apr–end Sep daily 7–6 (Oct–end Mar until 5). Treasury Apr–end Sep daily 9–6 (Oct–end Mar until 5)

🏪 Shop

Ⓜ Ottaviano

🚌 64 to Porta Cavalleggeri or 23, 32, 49, 492, 990 to Piazza del Risorgimento

♿ Wheelchair access

🎫 Basilica free. Dome and Treasury moderate. Grottos expensive

HIGHLIGHTS

● Façade
● Dome
● *Pietà*, Michelangelo
● *Baldacchino*, Bernini
● *St. Peter*, Arnolfo di Cambio
● Tomb of Paul III, Guglielmo della Porta
● Tomb of Urban VIII, Bernini
● Monument to Alexander VII, Bernini

Although some of the works of art in St. Peter's can be rather disappointing, the interior impresses as the spiritual capital of Roman Catholicism with an overwhelming sense of scale and decorative splendour.

The creators The first St. Peter's was built by Constantine around AD326, reputedly on the site where St. Peter was buried following his crucifixion in AD64. Between 1506 and 1626, it was virtually rebuilt to plans by Bramante, and then again to designs by Antonio da Sangallo, Giacomo della Porta, Michelangelo and Carlo Maderno. Michelangelo was also responsible for much of the dome, and Bernini finished the façade and the interior.

What to see Michelangelo's unforgettable *Pietà* (1499)— which is behind glass following an attack in 1972—is in the first chapel of the right nave. At the end of the same nave stands a statue of St. Peter: His right foot has been caressed by millions since 1857 when Pius IX granted a 50-day indulgence to anyone kissing it following confession. Bernini's high altar canopy, or *baldacchino* (1624–33), was built during the papacy of Urban VIII, a scion of the Barberini family; it is decorated with bees, the Barberini's dynastic symbol. To its rear are Guglielmo della Porta's Tomb of Paul III (left) and Bernini's influential Tomb of Urban VIII (right). Rome seen from the dome (entrance at the end of the right nave) is *the* highlight of a visit.

Castel Sant'Angelo

The route to the forti-
fied castle, Ponte
Sant'Angelo, watched
over by Bernini's angels

Castel Sant'Angelo, rising above the river, has served as an army barracks, papal citadel, imperial tomb and medieval prison. Today the 58-room museum traces the castle's near 2,000-year history, providing a contrast to the Vatican Museums.

Many incarnations The Castel Sant'Angelo was built by Emperor Hadrian in AD130 as a mausoleum for himself, his family and his dynastic successors. It was crowned by a gilded chariot driven by a statue of Hadrian disguised as the sun god Apollo. Emperors were buried in its vaults until about AD271, when under threat of invasion from Germanic raiders it became a citadel and was incorporated into the city's walls. Its present name arose in AD590, after a vision by Gregory the Great, who while leading a procession through Rome to pray for the end of plague saw an angel sheathing a sword on this spot, an act thought to symbolize the end of the pestilence.

Castle and museum In AD847 Leo IV converted the building into a papal fortress, and in 1277 Nicholas III linked it to the Vatican by a passageway, the *passetto*. A prison in the Renaissance, and then an army barracks after 1870, the castle became a museum in 1933. Exhibits, spread over four floors, are scattered around a confusing but fascinating array of rooms and corridors. Best of these is the beautiful Sala Paolina, done with stucco, fresco and *trompe-l'oeil*. The most memorable sight is the 360-degree view from the castle's terrace, the setting for the last act of Puccini's Tosca.

THE BASICS

🔲 E4
✉ Lungotevere Castello 50
☎ 06 681 9111
🕐 Tue–Sun 9–7.30
🍴 Café
🚇 Lepanto
🚌 30, 49, 70, 87, 130, 186, 224, 492, 926, 990 to Piazza Cavour or the Lungotevere
♿ Poor
💶 Expensive

HIGHLIGHTS

● Spiral funerary ramp
● Staircase of Alexander VI
● Armoury
● Hall of Justice
● Chapel of Leo X: façade by Michelangelo
● Sale di Clemente VII with wall paintings
● Cortile del Pozzo: wellhead
● Prisons (Prigione Storiche)
● Sala Paolina
● View from Loggia of Paul III

Musei Vaticani & Cappella Sistina

HIGHLIGHTS

- Sistine Chapel
- Laocoön
- Apollo del Belvedere (Museo Pio-Clementino)
- *Marte di Todi* (Museo Gregoriano-Etrusco)
- Maps Gallery (Galleria delle Carte Geografiche)
- Frescos by Pinturicchio
- Frescos by Fra Angelico
- Stanze di Raffaello
- Pinacoteca
- Room of the Animals (Museo Pio-Clementino)

TIPS

- Follow one of the colour-coded walks to ease your way through the crowds.
- Decide on your own priorities, choosing between the collections according to your interest.

The largest, richest and most impressive museum complex in the world incorporating one of Michelangelo's most supreme masterpieces in the Sistine Chapel.

Treasures of 12 museums At least two days (and 7km/4 miles of walking) are needed to do justice to the Vatican Museums. Egyptian and Assyrian art; Etruscan artefacts; the more esoteric anthropological collections; or modern religious art—whatever your priorities, several sights should not be missed. Most obvious are the four rooms of the Stanze di Raffaello, each of which is decorated with frescos by Raphael. Further fresco cycles by Pinturicchio and Fra Angelico adorn the Borgia Apartment and Chapel of Nicholas V, and are complemented by an almost unmatched collection of paintings in the Vatican Art Gallery. The

Galleria della Carte Geografiche decorated with 16th-century map frescos (far left and bottom left). Michelangelo's masterpiece, the ceiling of the Sistine Chapel (left, right and bottom right). An exhibit at the Vatican Museum (bottom middle)

best of the Greek and Roman sculpture is the breathtaking Laocoön group in the Cortile Ottagono of the Museo Pio-Clementino. The list of artists whose work is shown in the Collezione di Arte Religiosa Moderna is a roll call of the most famous in the last 100 years, from Pablo Picasso to Salvador Dalí and Henry Moore.

Sistine Chapel Built by Pope Sixtus IV between 1475 and 1483, Pope Julius II commissioned Michelangelo to paint the ceiling of the Sistine Chapel in 1508. The frescos, comprising over 300 individual figures, were completed in four years, during which Michelangelo worked in appalling conditions, lying on his back and in extremes of heat and cold. The extraordinary fresco behind the high altar, the *Last Judgment*, was begun for Pope Paul III in 1534 and completed in 1541.

THE BASICS

www.vatican.va

➕ C3

✉ Viale Vaticano, Città del Vaticano

☎ 06 6988 3322

🕐 Mar–end Oct Mon–Fri 8.45–4.45, Sat and last Sun of month 8.45–1.45; Nov–end Feb Mon–Sat and last Sun of month 8.45–1.45. Closed holidays

🍴 Café, restaurant and shop

🚇 Cipro–Musei Vaticani

🚌 23, 32, 49, 81, 492, 990 to Piazza del Risorgimento, 40 to Piazza Pia or 64 to Porta Cavalleggeri

♿ Wheelchair access

💷 Very expensive (includes entry to all Vatican museums); free last Sun of month

Shopping

CASTRONI

Castroni boasts Rome's largest selection of imported delicacies, a mouthwatering array of Italian specialties and an amazing range of coffees.
🞣 D3 ✉ Via Cola di Rienzo 196, corner of Via Terenzio ☎ 06 687 4383 🕐 Mon–Sat 8–8

MERCATO ANDREA DORIA

A large, local market that serves the area northwest of the Vatican. Stands mostly sell meat, fish, fruit and vegetables, but there are a few with shoes and quality clothes.
🞣 B3 ✉ Via Andrea Doria-Via Tunisi 🕐 Mon–Sat 7am–1pm

PIETRO FRANCHI

A rival to nearby Castroni as Rome's best delicatessen. Offers a selection of regional food and wines, and dishes to take out—anything from cold antipasti to succulent roast meats.
🞣 D3 ✉ Via Cola di Rienzo 204 ☎ 06 686 4576 🕐 Mon–Sat 8am–9pm

RELIGIOUS ARTEFACTS

For religious art and souvenirs, both serious and light-hearted, you should head to the streets around St. Peter's, notably Borgo Pio, Via del Mascherano and Via Porta di Porta Angelica.

Restaurants

PRICES

Prices are approximate, based on a 3-course meal for one person.
€€€   over €50
€€   €30–€50
€   under €30

BORGO NUOVO (€€)

This place is ideal after a visit to the Basilica or the Vatican museums for a quiet sit down and some tasty, freshly prepared Italian food.
🞣 D4 ✉ Borgo Pio 104 ☎ 06 689 2852 🕐 Wed–Mon 12–10 🚇 Ottaviano 🚌 81 to Piazza del Risorgimento

DAL TOSCANO (€)

This large *trattoria* in Vatican City serves Tuscan food, and is particularly known for its meats and its wood-fired grill.
🞣 C3 ✉ Via Germanico 58 ☎ 06 3972 5717 🕐 Tue–Sun 12.30–2.30, 7.30–11 🚇 Ottaviano 🚌 23, 49, 81 to Piazza del Risorgimento

COFFEE

Breakfast in Rome is washed down with a cappuccino or the longer and milkier *caffè latte*. At other times espresso, a short kick-start of caffeine, is the coffee of choice or *caffé macchiato*, with a drop of milk—Italians never drink cappuccino after lunch or dinner. Decaffeinated coffee is *caffè Hag* and iced coffee *caffé freddo*.

TAVERNA ANGELICA (€€)

Popular restaurant, the best mid-priced option in the area. Minimalist interior and delicate and innovative cooking.
🞣 D4 ✉ Piazza Amerigo Capponi 6 ☎ 06 687 4514 🕐 Mon–Sat 7–midnight, Sun 12.30–2.30, 7.30–midnight; closed 2 weeks Aug 🚇 Ottaviano 🚌 23 to Via San Porcari or to Piazza del Risorgimento

ZEN SUSHI (€€€)

Minimalist Japanese restaurant. Select tempting dishes from the constantly replenished conveyor belt.
🞣 D3 ✉ Via degli Scipioni 243 ☎ 06 321 3420 🕐 Tue–Fri 1–3, 6.30–11, Sat 7.30–11 🚇 Lepanto 🚌 30

If you're short of time, you can join an organized tour to enjoy some of the popular day trips from Rome. However, places such as the ancient ruins at Ostia Antica, can easily be made using public transport.

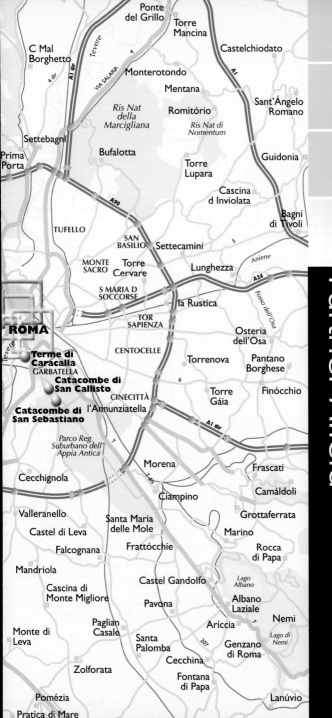

Ponte
del Grillo

Torre
Mancina

Castelchiodato

C Mal
Borghetto

Tevere

VIA SALARA

Monterotondo

Mentana

A1

Sant'Ángelo
Romano

Ris Nat
della
Marcigliana

Romitório

Ris Nat di
Nomentum

Settebagni

Bufalotta

Guidonia

Prima
Porta

Torre
Lupara

Cascina
d Inviolata

A90

Bagni
di Tívoli

TUFELLO

SAN
BASILIO

Settecamini

S

Aniene

MONTE
SACRO

Torre
Cervare

Lunghezza

A24

S MARIA D
SOCCORSE

Fosso dell'Osa

la Rustica

ROMA

TOR
SAPIENZA

Tevere

CENTOCELLE

Osteria
dell'Osa

Terme di
Caracalla

GARBATELLA

Torrenova

Pantano
Borghese

Catacombe di
San Callisto

6

CINECITTÀ

Torre
Gáia

Finócchio

Catacombe di
San Sebastiano

l'Annunziatella

A1 dir

Parco Reg
Suburbano dell'
Appia Antica

7

Morena

Frascati

Cecchignola

7 dir

Ciampino

Camáldoli

Valleranello

Santa Maria
delle Mole

Grottaferrata

Castel di Leva

Marino

Falcognana

Frattócchie

Rocca
di Papa

Mandriola

Castel Gandolfo

Lago
Albano

Cascina di
Monte Migliore

Pavóna

Albano
Laziale

Nemi

Monte di
Leva

Paglian
Casalè

Aríccia

Lago di
Nemi

Santa
Palomba

207

Genzano
di Roma

Zolforata

Cecchina

Fontana
di Papa

Pomézia

Lanúvio

Pratica di Mare

Ostia Antica

HIGHLIGHTS

● Decumanus Maximus
● Piazzale delle Corporazioni
● The Insule and Forum
● The Borgo

TIPS

● Allow a whole day for the site, perhaps bring a picnic.
● In summer, take water with you and rest in the shade during the early afternoon.
● Buy a plan of the site and spend time when you arrive planning your visit.

Ancient Rome's port is one of the top three best-preserved Roman towns in Italy, and is a haven of romantic ruins and soothing greenery.

Living in the past Untrumpeted Ostia Antica, 25km (15 miles) southwest of Rome, is Italy's best-preserved Roman town after Pompeii and Herculaneum, and its extensive ruins and lovely rural site are as appealing as any in Rome itself. Built at the mouth (*ostium*) of the Tiber as ancient Rome's seaport, it became a vast and bustling colony before silt and the Empire's decline together hastened its demise. By the 17th century Ostia Antica was all but forgotten. Roman legend puts Ostia's founding in the seventh century BC; factual dating of the ruins points to the fourth century BC.

The well-preserved amphitheatre, a major part of this archaeological site (left and bottom right). An intact fragment of wall decoration (bottom far left). Excavations, some more intact than others (bottom left and middle). A surviving mosaic (right)

Excavations Archaeological excavations began in the 19th century, and today about half the town has been uncovered, with some low-key excavations still continuing. Among the many excavated buildings are countless *horrea*, or warehouses, and several multistorey apartment blocks known as *insulae*. Other highlights include the Piazzale delle Corporazioni (the old business district) and the 4,000-seat amphitheatre.

Lovely picture Ostia is a quintessentially romantic classical ruin, complete with umbrella pines, grassy slopes and spreads of wildflowers. These certainly contribute to its evocative allure, but they make its preservation a nightmare, damaging walls and foundations. The size and scale of Ostia are more impressive by far than the capital's Forum, and it gives far better idea of ancient Roman life.

THE BASICS

www.itnw.roma/ostia
✚ Off map
✉ Viale di Romagnoli 717
☎ 06 5635 8099
🕐 Apr–end Sep, Tue–Sun 9–6; Oct–end Mar, Tue–Sun 8.30–4 (last admission 60–90 min before closing). Closed holidays
🍴 Restaurant
Ⓜ Metro line B to Piramide, then trains from adjoining Roma–Lido train station every 10–30 minutes (covered by BIG ticket ▷ 119)
💷 Moderate

More to See

CATACOMBE DI SAN CALLISTO

www.catacombe.roma.it

These catacombs are the largest and most impressive in Rome—and thus the most popular. They extend over 20km (12 miles) on five levels, with over 170,000 burial places. You can explore claustrophobic tunnels and numerous *loculi*, or burial niches, carved from the soft tufa stone.

🞢 Off map at J9 ✉ Via Appia Antica 110 ☎ 06 5130 1580 🕔 Thu–Tue 8.30–12, 2.30–5.30 (5 in winter). Closed Feb 🚌 118, 628 to Via delle Terme di Caracalla 🛗 Moderate

CATACOMBE DI SAN SEBASTIANO

The accessibility of the catacombs of San Sebastiano, once a 1st-century BC pagan cemetery, has made them vulnerable to pillage over the years. They were some of the most important burial places in early Christian Rome, and may even have housed the bodies of saints Peter and Paul.

🞢 Off map at K9 ✉ Via Appia Antica 136 ☎ 06 785 0350 🕔 Mon–Sat 8.30–12, 2.30–5.30 (5 in winter). Closed part of Nov and Dec 🚌 118, 628 to Via delle Terme di Caracalla 🛗 Moderate

TERME DI CARACALLA

Rome's most luxurious baths that could hold as many as 1,600 bathers. Started by Septimius Severus in AD206, and completed 11 years later by his son, Caracalla, they were designed as much as a gathering place as for hygiene. The site is now best known as a stage for outdoor opera.

🞢 J9 ✉ Via delle Terme di Caracalla 52 ☎ 06 3996 7700 🕔 Tue–Sun 9–1 hour before sunset, Mon 9–2; closed holidays 🚇 Circo Massimo 🚌 60, 75, 81, 175, 673 to Via di San Gregorio-Via delle Terme di Caracalla 🛗 Moderate (combined Appia Antica card gives admission to tombs on Via Appia Antica)

VILLA DORIA PAMPHILJ

If you have time to spare, and fancy a good long walk away from the crowds, there is nowhere better than this huge area of parkland.

🞢 B8 ✉ Via di San Pancrazio 🕔 Dawn–dusk 🚌 44, 75, 870 to the Gianicolo or 115, 125 to Via Garibaldi

The finest baths ever built in Rome, Terme di Caracalla

Laid out in 1650, the gardens of Villa Doria Pamphilj

Excursions

FRASCATI

Frascati is the loveliest of the Castelli Romani towns of the Colli Albani hills, famous for its wine and dominated by a majestic villa and its gardens.

The grandest of Frascati's villas is the Villa Aldobrandini, designed in 1598 by Giacomo della Porta. The vast palace, all faded majesty, is surrounded by a superb example of an early baroque garden, from where there are fabulous views. The town is scattered with other palaces and the baroque cathedral is notable, but leave time to sample the local wine. Made here since the 3rd century BC, Frascati is a worldwide seller; it's a revelation to drink it in its birthplace.

THE BASICS

Distance 20km (12 miles)
Journey time 40 min
🚆 Train from Termini
🚌 COTRAL bus from Anagnina metro station Villa Aldobrandini
✉ Via Cardinale Massaia
🕐 Garden only Apr–end Nov, Mon–Fri 9–1, 3–6; Dec–end Mar, Mon–Fri 9–1, 3–4

TIVOLI

Tivoli is the most popular excursion from Rome, thanks to the town's lovely wooded position, the superlative gardens of the Villa d'Este and the ruins and grounds of Hadrian's Roman villa.

The Este gardens were laid out in 1550 as part of a country retreat for Cardinal Ippolito d'Este, son of Lucrezia Borgia and the Duke of Ferrara. The highlights among the beautifully integrated terraces and many fountains are Gian Lorenzo Bernini's elegant Fontana di Bicchierone and the vast Viale delle Cento Fontane ('Avenue of the Hundred Fountains'). Hadrian's Villa (Villa Adriana) is an exceptional complex of Classical buildings, the largest ever conceived in the Roman world. It was built between AD118 and AD135 by Emperor Hadrian as an imperial palace away from the city and covered an area as great as the middle of imperial Rome.

THE BASICS

Distance 31km (19 miles)
Journey time 40 min
🚆 Train from Termini
🚌 COTRAL bus from Via Gaeta or metro line B to Ponte Mammolo and then COTRAL bus to Tivoli
Villa d'Este
✉ Piazza Trento
☎ 0424 600 460
🕐 Tue–Sun 8.30–4/7.30
💰 Expensive
Villa Adriana
✉ Via di Villa Adriana–Via Tiburtina
☎ 0774 530 203
🕐 Apr–end Jan 9–5
🚌 Local bus 4 or 4x from Tivoli 💰 Moderate

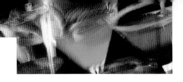

Entertainment and Nightlife

ALEXANDERPLATZ
www.alexanderplatz.it
A restaurant and cocktail bar north of St. Peter's with live jazz.
🚫 Off map ✉ Via Ostia 9 ☎ 06 3974 2171 🕐 Sep–Jun, Mon–Sat 9-2 🚇 Ottaviano 🚌 29N, 30N, 99N and 23, 70, 490, 913, 991, 994, 999 to Largo Trionfale-Viale delle Milizie 🎵 4-month membership (expensive); usually free to tourists (passport required)

PIPER
Open since the 1960s, Piper is consistently popular, thanks partly to its schedule of constant updating.
🚫 L1 ✉ Via Tagliamento 9 ☎ 06 855 5398 or 06 841 4459 🕐 Hours erratic. Sat and Sun only in winter 🚌 63, 86, 92, N29, N30 to Via Tagliamento 🎵 Very expensive

STADIO OLIMPICO
Home to Rome's two big football (soccer) teams, AS Roma and Lazio. Games are played here on alternate Sundays.
🚫 Off map ✉ Viale dei Gladiatori ☎ 06 323 7333 (box office) or 06 36851 🚌 32, 48, 69, 220, 225, 271, 280, 911 to Lungotevere Maresciallo Cadorna

AS Roma information:
Tickets available at many outlets around Rome. A full list is available on the official AS Roma website at www.asromacalcio.it. Also from Lottomatica stores and the AS Roma shop (✉ Via Colonna 360 ☎ 06 678 6514)

Lazio information:
Tickets can be bought online at www.sslazio.it. Also at Lottomatica stores or Lazio point at ✉ Via Farini ☎ 34 06 482 6768

Restaurants

PRICES

Prices are approximate, based on a 3-course meal for one person.
€€€   over €50
€€   €30–€50
€   under €30

ADRIANO (€€)
www.hoteladriano.it
Large restaurant and hotel in a 19th-century *palazzo*, with the same family since 1930. Classic and innovative Roman cooking, and alfresco dining during good weather.
🚫 Off map ✉ Via Villa Adriano 194, Tivoli ☎ 0774 382 235 🕐 Daily 12.30–2.30, 7–10.30 (closed Sun 7–10.30 winter)

CACCIANI (€€)
www.cacciani.it
In business for over half a century, serving Roman and classic Italian dishes. Lovely terrace with views as far as Rome. Try the house specialty, *pollo all Romana* (chicken in the Roman manner).
🚫 Off map ✉ Via A. Diaz 13, Frascati ☎ 06 942 0378 🕐 Tue–Sun 12.30–2.30, 7–10.30; closed Sun evening Oct–end May

IL GROTTINO DELLA SIBILLA DAL 1826 (€)
Well-priced, simple and tasty regional food presented in two intimate dining rooms (with a terrace for summer dining). The wine and olive oil used is home-produced.
🚫 Off map ✉ Piazza Rivarola 21, Tivoli ☎ 06774 433 2606 🕐 Daily 12.30–2.30, 7–10

ZARAZZÀ (€)
Appealing terrace plus three attractive dining rooms. Traditional Roman cooking with a light touch.
🚫 Off map ✉ Via Regina Margherita 45, Frascati ☎ 06 6942 2053 0378 🕐 Tue–Sun 12.30–2.30, 7–10.30 (closed Sun 7–10.30 Oct–end May and part of Aug)

Rome has a vast range of hotels in every price category, including some of Italy's most prestigious establishments. Many hotels are over-priced and poorly located; if you are on a short visit it pays to choose a hotel in or close to the historic area.

Introduction

Following Rome's renaissance in the wake of the Jubilee Year in 2000, the number of luxury five-star hotels in the city is now almost double what it was. Previously crumbling *palazzi* and many of the longer-established hotels have been restored.

Location, Location

As in any city, Rome has a wide range of accommodation types, from small, low-budget places around the Termini to grand, five-star luxury establishments on the Via Veneto. What to expect in terms of price and quality depends largely on location. Staying in the *centro storico* means that you are close to all of Rome's sights, but also to its sounds. Narrow streets and tall buildings tend to amplify the noise. Quiet places can be found, on the edge of the popular areas or in hotels with double glazing. If you really value your sleep, book a room in the quieter Aventino, Celio or Prati districts. The disadvantage here is that you will have to travel, but public transport is inexpensive, and hotels are often cheaper than in the heart of the city.

What you get for your Money

The familiar star system operates in Italy, with five stars denoting the highest standard of comfort, luxury and facilities. A one-star hotel has few facilities and frequently does not include a private bathroom. Normally both television and telephone will be in the lobby. These establishments tend not to accept credit cards and do not have a 24-hour desk service.

RESERVATIONS

As Rome is an eternally popular destination, it pays to reserve well in advance, especially if your stay is over the peak periods, which, nowadays, tend to be the greater part of the year. However, January to March and August are the least crowded months and you should be able to get some deals in this period. Consult hotel websites for details of special offers. If you arrive without a reservation, do ask to see the room first before you commit. Information agencies are always a useful resource.

After a hectic day sight-seeing, its nice to come back to a welcome smile and home comforts

Budget Hotels

PRICES

Expect to pay up to €100 per night for a double room in a budget hotel.

ABRUZZI

www.hotelabruzzi.it
Twenty-five large rooms (and eight shared bath-rooms), some with a view of the Pantheon; rooms at the rear are quieter.
✚ F5 ✉ Piazza della Rotonda 69 ☎ 06 679 2021; fax 06 6978 8076; 🚌 119 to Piazza della Rotonda or 46, 62, 63, 64, 70, 87, 186 to Largo di Torre Argentina

DELLA LUNETTA

www.albergodellalunetta.it
A plain 35-room hotel; it lacks panache but makes up for it with its position just off Campo de' Fiori.
✚ F6 ✉ Piazza del Paradiso 68 ☎ 06 686 1080; fax 06 689 2028 🚌 40, 64 and other services to Corso Vittorio Emanuele II

HOTEL TRASTEVERE

www.hoteltrastevere.net
One of only a few hotels in the Trastevere quarter. Twenty bright rooms, all with private bathrooms, plus 4 apartments.
✚ E7 ✉ Via Luciano Manara 24 ☎ 06 581 4713; fax 06 588 1016 🚌 H, 8, 780 to Piazza S. Sonnino or Viale Trastevere

KATTY

Less grim than most of the countless inexpensive hotels in the unsavoury area near Rome's train station. 28 rooms.
✚ L4 ✉ Via Palestro 35 ☎ 06 444 1216; fax 06 444 1216 🚇 Termini 🚌 64, 65, 170 and all other services to Termini

NAVONA

www.hotelnavona.com
Twenty-six simple rooms, friendly owners and a superb central location. Reserve well in advance.
✚ F5 ✉ Via dei Sediari 8 ☎ 06 686 4203; fax 06 6880 3802 🚌 30, 70, 87, 116, 186 to Corso del Rinascimento

PERUGIA

www.hperugia.it
Little-known, quiet and well placed between the Colosseum and Via Cavour; very convenient

NOISE

Noise is a fact of life in every Roman hotel, whatever the price category. Surveys have shown Rome to be the noisiest city in Europe. It is difficult to escape the cacophony entirely (unless the hotel is air-conditioned and windows are double-glazed), but to lessen the potential racket you should avoid rooms overlooking main thoroughfares and the area around Termini in favour of rooms looking out on parks or obscure back streets. Also ask for rooms away from the front of the hotel or facing on to a central courtyard (*cortile*).

for the sights of the Ancient City. All 11 doubles have private bathrooms.
✚ J6 ✉ Via del Colosseo 7 ☎ 06 679 7200; fax 06 678 4635 🚌 75, 84, 117 to Via Cavour or 75, 85, 87, 117, 175 to the Colosseum

POMEZIA

www.hotelpomezia.it
Close to Campo de' Fiori with 25 small rooms (some have private bathrooms). Roof terrace and small bar. Specially adapted room for people with disabilities.
✚ F6 ✉ Via dei Chiavari 12 ☎ 06 686 1371; fax 06 686 1371 🚌 46, 62, 64 to Corso Vittorio Emanuele II or 8, 46, 62, 63, 64, 70, 80 to Largo di Torre Argentina

SMERALDO

www.hotelsmeraldoroma.com
Thirty-five plain and clean rooms. In a back street close to Campo de' Fiori.
✚ F6 ✉ Vicolo dei Chiodaroli 11 ☎ 06 687 5929; fax 06 6880 5495 🚌 46, 62, 64 to Corso Vittorio Emanuele II or 8, 46, 62, 63, 64, 70, 80 to Largo di Torre Argentina

SOLE

www.solealbiscione.it
A popular choice on the edge of Campo de' Fiori with 59 rooms and a small garden terrace.
✚ F6 ✉ Via del Biscione 76 ☎ 06 6880 6873; fax 06 689 3787 🚌 46, 62, 64 to Corso Vittorio Emanuele II or 8, 46, 62, 63, 64, 70, 80 to Largo di Torre Argentina

Mid-Range Hotels

PRICES

Expect to pay between €100 and €250 per night for a double room in a mid-range hotel.

CAMPO DE' FIORI

www.hotelcampodefiori.com
Good value and position close to Campo de' Fiori. The 27 rooms are rather small and vary in decor, from exposed brick to funky blues. The roof garden is a pleasant bonus.
F6 ⊠ Via del Biscione 6 ☎ 06 6880 6865; fax 06 687 6003 🚌 46, 62, 64 to Corso Vittorio Emanuele II

CASA HOWARD

www.casahoward.com
The success of the first Casa Howard, a lovely residence close to Piazza di Spagna, spawned this second Casa Howard II, which opened in 2003. The five rooms all have private bathrooms. The location is excellent for shopping and the sights near the Spanish Steps and Fontana di Trevi.
G4 ⊠ Via Capo le Case 18 ☎ 06 6992 4555; fax 06 6794 6444 🚇 Spagna 🚌 116, 116T, 117, 119, 590 to Via dei Due Macelli or all services to Via del Tritone

CESARI

www.albergocesari.it
Friendly and straightforward three-star hotel with a loyal clientele and 47 elegant rooms that were renovated in 1999. Very

long-established—there has been a hotel here since 1787. Excellent position at the heart of the historic city.
G5 ⊠ Via di Pietra 89a ☎ 06 674 9701; fax 06 6749 7030 🚌 60, 62, 85, 117, 119, 160 to Via del Corso

COLUMBUS

www.hotelcolumbus.net
A converted monastery very close to St. Peter's—preferred by visiting cardinals. The 92 rooms are clean and functional, but the position is the hotel's real strength.
D4 ⊠ Via della Conciliazione 33 ☎ 06 686 5435; fax 06 686 4874 🚌 23, 34 to Via della Conciliazione or 64 to Piazza San Pietro

COMFORT INN BOLIVAR

www.bolivarhotel.com
This three-star hotel is perfectly positioned for sights of the Ancient City, in a quiet alley just off busy Via IV Novembre. 35 decent, modern rooms. Breakfast is taken

AGENCIES

Two good sources for all kinds of accommodation, from hotels to bed-and-breakfast in all price ranges, are the Hotel Reservation Agency (☎ 06 699 1000; www.hotelreservation.it) and Enjoy Rome (☎ 06 445 1843 or 06 445 0734; www.enjoyrome.com 🕐 Mon–Fri 8.30–7, Sat 8.30–2).

on the roof terrace.
H6 ⊠ Via della Cordonata 6, between Via IV Novembre and Via XXIV Maggio ☎ 06 679 1614; fax 06 679 1025 🚇 Cavour 🚌 H, 40, 60, 64, 70, 116T, 117, 170 to Via IV Novembre or Via Nazionale

DUE TORRI

www.hotelduetorriroma.com
A real find, in a perfect position hidden in a tiny alley between Piazza Navona and the Tiber. The 26 adequate rooms vary from stylish to plain. Some have small terraces with good views.
F5 ⊠ Vicolo del Leonetto 23–25 ☎ 06 687 6983; fax 06 686 5442 🚌 30, 70, 81, 87, 116, 186 to Lungotevere Marzio or Corso del Rinascimento

HOTEL PORTOGHESI

www.hotelportoghesiroma.com
A well-known hotel in a baroque *palazzo* with a roof terrace. Has been updated while retaining the 19th-century period feel of its 27 rooms. In a cobbled street north of Piazza Navona.
F4 ⊠ Via dei Portoghesi 1 ☎ 06 686 4231; fax 06 687 6976 🚌 30, 70, 87, 116 to Corso del Rinascimento

IL PICCOLO DI PIAZZA SPAGNA

www.piazzadispagna.com
A little-known three-star hotel in a small (*piccolo*) town house 300m southeast of Piazza di Spagna. It has 11 charming rooms, some with Jacuzzis, and a small

terrace where breakfast is served in fine weather.
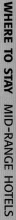 H4 ✉ Via dei Due Macelli 47 ☎ 06 6929 0847; fax 06 6920 0560 🚇 Spagna 🚌 116, 116T, 117, 119, 590 to Via dei Due Macelli or all services to Via del Tritone

LOCARNO
www.hotellocarno.com
In a quietish side street close to Piazza del Popolo. Much genuine 1920s art nouveau decor, but with a feel of old-world elegance plus nice touches such as an open fire in winter and a garden and roof terrace. Ask for the better rooms in the eastern annexe, not the downbeat rooms in the main building.
H F3 ✉ Via della Penna 22 ☎ 06 361 0841; fax 06 321 5249 🚇 Flaminio 🚌 926 to Via di Ripetta, or 81 to Lungotevere in Augusta

MANFREDI
www.hotelmanfredi.it
Quiet family-run hotel with charming service and 18 pretty rooms, in a cobbled street of galleries and antiques shops.
H G3 ✉ Via Margutta 61 ☎ 06 320 7676; fax 06 320 7736 🚇 Spagna 🚌 119 to Piazza di Spagna

NERVA
www.hotelnerva.com
Unbeatable position for the sights of the Ancient City—this is one of only a few hotels within a stone's throw of the Roman Forum. Renovated rooms, some with original

features, amiable service and a warm welcome.
H H6 ✉ Via Tor de'Conti 3 ☎ 06 678 1835; fax 06 6992 2204 🚇 Colosseo or Cavour 🚌 60, 84, 85, 87, 175 and all other services to Via dei Fori Imperiali, Piazza Venezia or Via IV Novembre-Via Nazionale

PONTE SISTO
www.hotelpontesisto.it
At the top end of the mid-range price, this four-star hotel is in a peaceful street just steps from the bridge to Trastevere. 106 simple rooms with fine marble bathrooms and a palm-lined courtyard.
H F6 ✉ Via dei Pettinari 64 ☎ 06 686 310; fax 06 6830 1712 🚌 23, 271, 280 to

RESERVATIONS
Rome's peak season runs from Easter to October, but the city's hotels (in all categories) are almost invariably busy. Telephone, write or fax well in advance to reserve a room (most receptionists speak some English, French or German). Leave a credit card number or send an international money order for the first night's stay to be certain of the booking. Reconfirm a few days before your trip. If you arrive without a reservation then get to a hotel early in the morning; by afternoon most vacated rooms will have been snapped up. Don't accept rooms from touts at Stazione Termini.

Lungotevere dei Vallati or H, 8, 63, 271, 630 to Via Arenula

LA RESIDENZA
www.hotel-la-residenza.com
Good choice, close to Via Vittorio Veneto (but away from the hustle and bustle) and reasonably priced for this expensive area. 26 airy and stylish rooms. Combines the luxury of a five-star hotel with the intimacy and easy going charm of a private house. Terrace and roof garden.
H H3 ✉ Via Emilia 22–24 ☎ 06 488 0789; fax 06 485721 🚇 Barberini 🚌 52, 53, 80, 95, 116, 119 to Via Vittorio Veneto

LA RESIDENZA FARNESE
www.residenzafarneseroma.it
A superb position in an ivy-hung alley and in the shadow of the great Palazzo Farnese. Part of a former convent, the rooms vary from modest former nuns' cells with small bathrooms to large, pastel-decorated salons.
H E6 ✉ Via del Mascherone 59 ☎ 06 6821 0980; fax 06 8032 1049 🚌 116, 116T to Via Giulia and Via dei Farnesi

SISTINA
www.leonardihotels.com
Small, efficient and close to the Piazza di Spagna. Lovely terrace for drinks and breakfast. 23 rooms.
H H4 ✉ Via Sistina 136 ☎ 06 474 4176; fax 06 481 8867 🚇 Spagna or Barberini 🚌 119 to Piazza di Spagna or 52, 53, 61, 62, 80, 95, 116, 119, 175 to Piazza Barberini

Luxury Hotels

ALBERGO DEL SOLE AL PANTHEON

www.hotelsolealpantheon.com
Chic and old—open since 1467. Opposite the Pantheon; if you can stand the crowds, the location is one of the best. 25 rooms.
➕ F5 ✉ Piazza della Rotonda 63 ☎ 06 678 0441; fax 06 6994 0689 🚌 119 to Piazza della Rotonda or 70, 87 to Corso del Rinascimento

AMBASCIATORI PALACE

www.ambasciatoripalace.com
One of the more venerable and stately of Via V. Veneto's large luxury hotels, with a traditional feel and opulent appearance. 110 rooms.
➕ H–J3 ✉ Via Vittorio Veneto 62 ☎ 06 47493; fax 06 474 3601 🚇 Barberini 🚌 52, 53, 95, 116, 119 to Via Vittorio Veneto

ATLANTE STAR

www.atlantehotels.com
Luxury hotel between Vatican City and the Castel Sant'Angelo exuding class and elegance.
➕ D4 ✉ Via G. Vitelleschi 34 ☎ 06 687 3233 🚇 Ottaviano 🚌 32, 81, 492

DE RUSSIE

www.roccofortehotels.com
A glorious hotel just off Piazza del Popolo that is distinguished by its modern and stylish design. The 123 rooms are calm and bright, and most have views of the delightful gardens, a lovely spot to dine alfresco.
➕ F3 ✉ Via del Babuino 9 ☎ 06 328 881; fax 3288 8888 🚇 Flaminio 🚌 117, 119 to Piazza del Popolo

HASSLER-VILLA MEDICI

www.hotelhasslerroma.com
Well-located longtime jet-set and VIP haunt, just above the Spanish Steps. 86 rooms and 13 suites.
➕ H4 ✉ Piazza Trinità dei Monti 6 ☎ 06 699 340; fax 06 678 9991 🚇 Spagna 🚌 119 to Piazza di Spagna

LORD BYRON

www.lordbyronhotel.com
Small, refined and very chic in leafy Parioli. Noted for its excellent restaurant Relais Le Jardin. 32 rooms, plus 3 suites.
➕ G1 ✉ Via Giuseppe de Notaris 5 ☎ 06 322 4541; fax 06 322 0405 🚇 Flaminio 🚌 52 to Via Bruno Buozzi

RAPHAEL

www.raphaelhotel.com
Intimate, charming and ivy covered—hidden away yet near Piazza Navona. The 73 rooms are a little small but immaculate. Reserve ahead.
➕ F5 ✉ Largo Febo 2 ☎ 06 682 831; fax 06 687 8993 🚌 70, 81, 87 to Corso del Rinascimento

ST. REGIS GRAND

www.stregis.com
Not in the most salubrious or convenient spot, but immensely lavish and luxurious. 138 rooms, plus 35 suites.
➕ K4 ✉ Via Vittorio Emanuele Orlando 3 ☎ 06 47091/474 709; fax 06 474 7307 🚇 Repubblica 🚌 H, 40, 170, 492, 910 to Piazza della Repubblica

WESTIN EXCELSIOR

www.westin.com
Large and grand: Everything is on an enormous scale, from the vast silk rugs to the 284 palatial bedrooms (32 suites).
➕ H–J3 ✉ Via Vittorio Veneto 125 ☎ 06 47081; fax 06 482 6205 🚇 Barberini 🚌 52, 53, 95, 116, 119 to Via Vittorio Veneto

Rome can be a busy and intimidating place, but behind the bustle it is easy to access the city from its two airports, while public transport, on the few occasions you will need it, is reliable and straightforward.

Need to Know

Planning Ahead

When to Go

The best time to visit Rome is April to early June or mid-September to October, when the weather is not uncomfortably hot. Easter weekend is very busy. Many restaurants and businesses close for the entire month of August. January and February are the quietest months.

TIME

Italy is one hour ahead of GMT in winter, six hours ahead of New York and nine hours ahead of Los Angeles.

AVERAGE DAILY MAXIMUM TEMPERATURES											
JAN	FEB	MAR	APR	MAY	JUN	JUL	AUG	SEP	OCT	NOV	DEC
44°F	46°F	52°F	58F	64°F	74°F	79°F	77°F	72°F	64°F	55°F	48°F
7°C	8°C	11°C	14°C	18°C	23°C	26°C	25°C	22°C	18°C	13°C	9°C

Spring (March to April) can be muggy and rainy in April and May.
Summer (June to August) is hot and dry, with sudden thunderstorms. July and August are uncomfortably hot.
Autumn (September to November) is mixed but can produce crisp days with clear skies.
Winter (December to February) is short and cold.

WHAT'S ON

January *La Befana* (6 Jan): Epiphany celebrations; fair and market in Piazza Navona.
February *Carnevale* (week before Lent): Costume festivities; parties on Shrove Tuesday.
March *Festa di San Giuseppe* (19 Mar): Street stalls in the Trionfale area north of the Vatican.
April *Good Friday* (Mar/Apr): Procession of the Cross at 9pm to the Colosseum, led by the Pope.
Easter Sunday: The Pope addresses the crowds at noon in Piazza di San Pietro.

May *International Horse Show* (early May): Concorso Ippico in Villa Borghese.
June *Festa della Repubblica* (2 Jun): Military parade along Via de' Fiori Imperiali.
July *Tevere Expo* (last week Jun/Jul): Food and handicrafts fair on the banks of the Tiber.
August *Ferragosto* (15 Aug): Feast of the Assumption; everything closes.
September *Art Fair*: Via Margutta.
Sagra dell'Uva (early Sep): Wine and harvest festival in the Basilica di Massenzio.

October *Antiques Fair* (mid-Oct): Via dei Coronari.
November *Ognissanti* (1–2 Nov): All Saints' Day.
Festa di Santa Cecilia (22 Nov): In the catacombs and church of Santa Cecilia in Trastavere.
December *Festa della Madonna Immacolata* (8 Dec): Pope and other dignitaries leave flowers at the statue of the Madonna in Piazza di Spagna.
Christmas Eve Midnight Mass: Most striking are at Santa Maria Maggiore and Santa Maria in Aracoeli.

Useful Websites

www.romaturismo.it
Rome's official website for tourist information, has mostly generalized information on the city.

www.adr.it
The official site of Rome's main airports, Fiumincino and Ciampino, with useful contacts and details of transport links to the city.

www.vatican.va
Vatican City's polished official website offers multilingual information on the Musei Vaticani, a calendar of religious events, an online version of its official newspaper and other general information on the Vatican.

www.comune.roma.it
Aimed primarily at tourists, the official website of Rome's city council contains transport and other useful general information.

www.romaclick.com
A general site useful for checking up-to-the-minute information on events and exhibitions. It offers a user-friendly accommodation reservation service with last-minute reductions.

www.romeguide.it
An Italian-based site with a wealth of daily updated information; use it for reserving museum passes and to find out what's on.

www.enjoyrome.com
This friendly English-language site is run from Rome and has a quirkier approach than most; use it for general information, as well as tips on discovering Rome on foot and by public transport. Excellent links and daily updates.

www.museionline.it
Informative and easy-to-navigate site that will fill you in on what the city's museums have to offer. Lots of practical information as well. Opening times and prices are not always current.

PRIME TRAVEL SITES

www.atac.roma.it
Rome's bus company website gives every scrap of information about public transport, including maps and how to buy the best ticket for your needs—Italian and English.

www.capitolium.org
Devoted to the Roman Forum and the Imperial Fora, this site includes a wide range of historical material, including reconstructions of how the Fora might have looked in its original state.

www.catacombe.roma.it
The official site of Rome's catacombs.

www.fodors.com
A travel-planning site where you can research prices and weather, book tickets, cars and rooms, and ask questions; links to other sites.

CYBERCAFÉS

easyInternetcafe
www.easyinternetcafe.com
✉ H4 ✉ Via Barberini 2
🕐 Daily 7am–1am

Globalservice
✉ F7 ✉ Piazza S. Sonnino
27 ☎ 06 5833 3316
🕐 Daily 8am–midnight

Getting There

VISAS AND INSURANCE

Check visa and passport requirements before travelling, see www.britishembassy.gov.uk or www.american embassy.com. EU citizens are covered for medical expenses with an EHIC card; insurance to cover illness and theft is still strongly advised. Visitors from outside the EU should check their insurance coverage and, if necessary, buy a supplementary policy.

TIPS

● Avoid taxi and hotel touts who will approach you at the airport. Use only licensed (yellow or white) taxis.
● Buy your return (round-trip) train ticket when you arrive at Fiumicino. The queues are much longer at Termini, and the ticket will not become valid until you stamp it on your return journey.
● You will find suitcases with wheels a godsend at Fiumicino. It is quite some distance between baggage reclaim and the exit, and for some stretches you cannot use a baggage trolley, particularly on the homeward journey.

AIRPORTS

There are direct flights into Rome from Europe and North America to Leonardo da Vinci and Ciampino airports. Visitors from Europe can also arrive by rail to Stazione Termini, or by bus.

60KM (37 miles)

✕ **Leonardo da Vinci Airport**
36km (22 miles) to city centre
Train 45 min, €9.50

✕ **Ciampino Airport**
15km (9 miles) to city centre
Bus/Metro 35 min

FROM LEONARDO DA VINCI

Scheduled flights arrive at this airport 36km (22 miles) southwest of the city, better known as Fiumicino (☎ switchboard 06 65951, 24hr recorded 06 6593 3640, flight information 06 6563 4956 (international), 06 65643 (domestic). The website for both main Rome airports is www.adr.it. The most economical way to reach the heart of Rome from the airport is by rail into Stazione Termini. Trains leave every 30 or 60 minutes (6.37am–11.37pm) at 7 and 37 minutes past the hour and take about 35 minutes. Buses depart outside train hours and take up to 50 minutes to Rome's Termini and Tiburtina train stations. Taxis take from 30 minutes to two hours depending on traffic, and are expensive (€40–€55). Take only licensed cabs (white or yellow) or a prepaid car with driver available from the SOCAT desk in the International Arrivals hall.

FROM CIAMPINO

This smaller airport, which handles mostly low-cost and charter flights, is 15km (9 miles) southeast of the city. There are good facilities but the airport doesn't have a direct rail link to

the heart of Rome. To get there take a 15-minute bus journey by COTRAL bus to the Metro (underground) station at Anagnina, then the 20-minute journey to Termini on Metro line A. Taxis take between 30 and 40 minutes and cost around €40. Bus shuttles (☎ 06 7949 4572; www.terravision.it) serve various no-frills and other airlines' flights and run to Termini (€8 one-way, €14 round-trip). Terravision also operates from Fiumicino airport to Termini (€7 one-way, €12 round-trip).

ARRIVING BY BUS
Most long-distance buses terminate at Tiburtina, to the northeast of the city. Although the station is somewhat way out of the city, it is well served by the Metro (line B) and by numerous bus services (for example. No. 492). Eurolines run buses from more than 100 European cities. For details of routes and tickets, see their website (www.eurolines.com).

ARRIVING BY CAR
In the days of the empire, all roads led to Rome, but in these modern times, all roads lead to the Gran Raccordo Anulare, known as the GRA. This 70km (43-mile) road encircles the city, and is always busy. From Fiumicino airport, take the Autostrada Roma Fiumicino, which leads to the GRA. If you are coming from Ciampino you will need to follow the Via Appia Nuova. From Florence or Pisa, take the A1, also known as the Autostrada del Sole. Visitors arriving from Naples should also use the A1, while those coming from Abruzzo or the Adriatic coast should follow the A24. Wherever you join the GRA, make sure you know which exit you need; your hotel can tell you which one is best.

ARRIVING BY RAIL
Most trains arrive and depart from Stazione Termini, which is convenient for most of central Rome. Taxis and buses leave from the station forecourt, Piazza dei Cinquecento. Train information ☎ 8488 88088; www.trenitalia.com.

DRIVING PERMIT
If you are arriving by car and staying in central Rome, you will need a permit to drive in the city. If you are staying in a hotel, the staff can arrange this.

LONG-TERM PARKING
If you are arriving by car, but don't want to use your car in Rome, you can leave it in the long-term parking area (*lungo sosta parcheggio*) at Fiumicino airport and take the train into the city. Parking costs €18 for 24 hours or €69 for seven days. Short-stay costs €28 daily (☎ 06 6595 5175).

CAR RENTAL
All major rental firms, and some local ones, have desks at both airports and also in town. Car rental is expensive in Italy and you can often get a better deal if you arrange it before you leave home. The minimum age for renting a car is between 21 and 25 (depending on which company), and you will need a have held a driver's licence for a least a year. Most firms require a credit card as a deposit. Accidents rates are high in Rome, so make sure you have adequate insurance cover. Most car rental contracts include breakdown cover.

Getting Around

AMERICAN EXPRESS

American Express runs bus tours around Rome and farther afield. It also organizes three- to four-hour walks of the city with English-speaking guides. Reserve ahead at busy times (✉ Piazza di Spagna 38 ☎ 06 67642 🕓 Apr–end Sep, Mon–Fri 9–5.30, Sat 9–3; Oct–end Mar, Mon–Fri 9–5.30, Sat 9–12.30 🚌 119 to Piazza di Spagna).

VISITORS WITH DISABILITIES

Rome is not an easy place for visitors with physical disabilities. However, Vatican City has ramps and elevators and some hotels have rooms for visitors with disabilities. Staff at airports, museums and places of interest are willing to help and taxis usually accept wheel-chairs, although it is a good idea to phone ahead. The B line Metro is generally accessible (apart from Circo Massimo, Colosseo and Cavour) but the A line and most buses are not. For details contact RADAR (✉ Unit 12, City Forum, 250 City Road, London ECU 8AF ☎ 020 7250 3222; www.radar.org.uk) in the UK or Society for the Advancement of Travel and Hospitality (SATH) (✉ 347 5th Avenue, Suite 610 NY 10016 ☎ 212/447 7284; www.sath.org) in the US.

BUSES

Service is frequent and inexpensive on Rome's orange, green or red-grey regional and blue suburban buses run by ATAC/COTRAL.

🚇 K4 ✉ Piazza dei Cinquecento ☎ 800 431784 (freephone) or 06 4695 2057; www.atac.roma.it 🕓 Mon–Fri 9–1, plus Tue and Fri 2.30–5 🚇 Termini

The buses are often crowded and slow. Buy BIT tickets (*Biglietto Integrato a Tempo*; €1) before boarding, available from tobacconists, automatic machines and shops displaying an ATAC sticker. Your ticket must be stamped at the rear of the bus or tram, and is valid for any number of bus rides and one Metro ride within the next 75 minutes. Day (€4) and three-day (€11) BTI passes are available. These need only be validated the first time they are used. There are large fines if you are caught without a ticket. Daytime services run from 5.30am to 11.30pm, depending on the route. The night service consists of buses on key routes from midnight to 5.30am; night buses have a conductor selling tickets. Remember to enter buses by back doors and to leave by middle doors (if you have a pass or validated ticket with unexpired time you can also use the front doors). Buy several tickets at once as some outlets close early or the 5-ticket 5BIT-Multibit pass (€5), which must be validated for each journey. There are large fines if you are caught without a ticket. Bus stops (*fermate*) list routes and bus numbers and note that one-way streets often force buses to return along different routes.

USEFUL SERVICES

● 23 Piazza del Risorgimento (for the Vatican Museums)–Trastevere–Piramide
● 75 Termini–Roman Forum–Colosseum–Piramide
● 40, 64 Termini–Piazza Venezia–close to Piazza San Pietro/St. Peter's
● 110 Sightseeing service from Stazione Termini and other key monuments
● 81 Piazza del Risorgimento (Vatican

Museums)–Piazza Venezia

● 117, 119 Circular minibus service in the historic centre: Piazza Augusto Imperatore–Piazza della Rotonda (Pantheon)–Via del Corso–Piazza di Spagna

● 780 Piazza Venezia–Trastevere

SUBWAY

Rome's subway, the Metro, has two lines, A and B, which intersect at Stazione Termini. Mainly a commuter service and of limited use in the city, it is good for trans-city rides. Station entrances are marked by a large M and each displays a map of the network. Services run 5.30am to 11.30pm (12.30am on Saturday). Tickets are valid for one ride and can be bought from tobacconists, bars and shops displaying ATAC or COTROL stickers, and from machines at stations.

TAXIS

Official taxis are yellow or white, with a 'Taxi' sign on the roof. Use only these and refuse touts at Fiumicino, Termini and elsewhere. Drivers are not supposed to stop on the streets so it is difficult to hail a cab. Taxis congregate at stands, indicated by blue signs printed with 'Taxi'. Make sure the meter is reset when you start your journey (note one part of the meter will display the minimum-fare starting rate). Ranks are available in the area at Termini, Piazza S Sonnino, Pantheon, Piazza di Spagna and Piazza San Silvestro.

Calling a taxi: the company will give you a taxi code name, a number and the time it will take to get to you. The meter starts running as soon as they are called. Companies include: Samaranda ☎ 06 5551; Autoradio Taxi ☎ 06 3570; Capitale Radio ☎ 06 4994. The minimum fare is valid for 3km (2.5 miles) or the first 9 minutes of a ride. Surcharges are levied between 10pm and 7am, all day Sunday, on national holidays, for airport trips and for each piece of luggage larger than 35 x 25 x 50cm (13 x 9 x 19in).

HANDY HINT

An integrated ticket, the *Biglietto Integrato Giornaliero* (BIG) is valid for a day's unlimited travel on ATAC buses, the Metro, COTRAL buses and suburban trains (except to Fiumicino airport). The *Carta Integrata Settimanale* pass (€16) is valid for a week as for BIG tickets (see above).

LOST PROPERTY

Report lost or stolen property to a police station, which will issue a signed declaration for your insurance company. The central police station is the Questura

✉ Via San Vitale 15

☎ 06 46861 (tourist department) or ☎ 06 4686 2102

ATAC lost property

✉ Via Niccolò Bettoni 1

☎ 06 581 6040

🕓 Mon–Sat 8.30–1

Metro lost property

Line A ☎ 06 487 4309;
Line B ☎ 06 5735 2264

🕓 Mon, Wed, Fri 9–12

COTRAL lost property

Inquire at the route's origin or telephone ☎ 06 57531 or 06 591 5551

Rail lost property

✉ Stazione Termini, Via Giovanni Giolitti 24 ☎ 06 4782 5543 🕓 Mon–Fri 7am–10pm

Airport lost property

☎ 06 6595 3343 🕓 Mon–Fri 9–1, also Thu 2–3.30

Essential Facts

NATIONAL HOLIDAYS

- 1 Jan (New Year's Day)
- 6 Jan (Epiphany)
- Easter Monday
- 25 Apr
- 1 May (Labour Day)
- 29 Jun (St. Peter & St. Paul's Day)
- 15 Aug (Assumption)
- 1 Nov (All Saints' Day)
- 8 Dec (Immaculate Conception
- 25 Dec (Christmas Day)
- 26 Dec (St. Stephen's Day)

MONEY

The euro is the official currency of Italy. Banknotes come in denominations of 5, 10, 20, 50, 100, 200 and 500 euros and coins in 1, 2, 5, 10, 20, 50 cents and 1 and 2 euros.

10 euros

50 euros

200 euros

500 euros

ELECTRICITY

- Current is 220 volts AC, 50 cycles; plugs are the two-round-pin type.

NEWSPAPERS & MAGAZINES

- Most Romans read the Rome-based *Il Messaggero*, the mainstream and authoritative *Corriere della Sera* or the middle-left and popularist *La Repubblica* (which has a special Rome edition). Sports papers (such as *Corriere dello Sport*) and news magazines (like *Panorama* and *L'Espresso*) are also popular.
- Foreign newspapers can usually be bought after 2.30pm on the day of issue from booths (*edicole*) on and close to Termini, Piazza Colonna, Largo di Torre Argentina, Piazza Navona, Via Vittoria Veneto and close to several tourist sights. European editions of the *International Herald Tribune*, *USA Today* and the *Financial Times* are also available.

OPENING HOURS

- Shops: Tue–Sat 8–1, 4–8, Mon 4–8 (with seasonal variations) or, increasingly Mon/Tue–Sat 9.30–7.30. Food shops open on Monday morning but may close on Thursday afternoon.
- Restaurants: daily 12.30–3, 7.30–10.30. Many close on Sunday evening and half- or all day Monday. Most bars and restaurants also have a statutory closing day (*riposo settimanale*) and many close for much of August.
- Churches: variable, but usually daily 7–12, 4.30–7. Most churches close Sunday afternoon.
- Museums and galleries: vary considerably; usually close on Monday.
- Banks: Mon–Fri 8.30–1.30. Major branches may also open 3–4 and Saturday morning.
- Post offices: Mon–Fri 8.15 or 9–2; Sat 8.15 or 9–12 or 2

POSTAL SERVICE

- Buy stamps from post offices and tobacconists.
- Post boxes are red and have two slots, one for Rome (marked *Per La Città*) and one for other destinations (*Per Tutte Le Altre*

Destinazioni). New boxes, usually blue, are for the priority mail service, or *Posta Priorita*.

● Vatican post can be posted only in the Vatican's blue *Poste Vaticane* post boxes. The Vatican postal service is quicker (although tariffs are the same), but stamps can be bought only at the post offices in the Vatican Museums 🕐 Mon–Fri 8.30–7 and in Piazza San Pietro ☎ 06 6988 3406 🕐 Mon–Fri 8.30–7, Sat 8.30–6

● Main post office (*Ufficio Postale Centrale*) ✉ Piazza San Silvestro 18–20 ☎ 06 6771; www.poste.it 🕐 Mon–Fri 9am–6.30/7.30pm, Sat 8.30–1 (9–12 last Sat of month).

TELEPHONES

● Telephone numbers listed in this book include the city area code (06), which must be dialled even when calling from within Rome.
● Public telephones are indicated by a red or yellow sign showing a telephone dial and receiver. They are found on the street, in bars and restaurants and in special offices (*Centri Telefoni*) equipped with banks of phones.
● Phones usually accept phone cards (*schede telefoniche*) available from tobacconists, post offices and some bars in a variety of denominations. Break off the card's corner before use.
● To call Italy from the UK, dial 00 44 and from the US or Canada dial 011, followed by 39 (the country code for Italy) then the number, including the relevant city code.

TOURIST INFORMATION

● Azienda di Promozione Turistica di Roma ✉ Via Parigi 11 and Via Parigi 5 ☎ 06 3600 4399 or 06 488 991 🕐 Mon– Sat 8am–7pm
● Information kiosks (daily 9–6) are at ✉ Largo Goldoni ☎ 06 6813 6061; ✉ Piazza Tempio della Pace ☎ 06 6992 4307; ✉ Piazza delle Cinque Lune ☎ 06 6880 9240; ✉ Palazzo delle Esposizioni, Via Nazionale ☎ 06 4782 4525; ✉ Piazza San Giovanni in Laterano ☎ 06 7720 3535; ✉ Lungotevere Castel Sant'Angelo-Piazza Pia ☎ 06 6880 9707

MEDICAL TREATMENT

There are emergency rooms at these centres: Ospedale Fatebenefratelli ✉ Isola Tiberina ☎ 06 683 7299/06 68371; Policlinico Umberto I ✉ Viale del Policlinico 155 ☎ 06 446 2341 or 06 49971; www.policlinicoumberto1.it. The George Eastman Clinic (✉ Viale Regina Elena 287/b ☎ 06 844 831) provides an emergency dentist service. No credit cards.

Pharmacies are indicated by a large green cross. Opening times are usually Mon–Sat 8.30–1, 4–8, but a rotating schedule (displayed on pharmacy doors) ensures at least one is open 24 hours a day, seven days a week. The most central English-speaking pharmacist is Internazionale (✉ Piazza Barberini 49 ☎ 06 482 5456).

EMERGENCY NUMBERS

Police, Fire and Ambulance (general SOS) ☎ 113
Police (Carabinieri) ☎ 112
Central Police ☎ 06 46861
UK Embassy ☎ 06 4220 0001
US Embassy ☎ 06 46741
Information ☎ 12
International information (Europe) ☎ 176
International information (rest of the world) ☎ 170
ACI Auto Assistance (car breakdowns) ☎ 116
General info-tourist line ☎ 06 8205 9127

Language

All Italian words are pronounced as written, with each vowel and consonant sounded. Only the letter *h* is silent, but it modifies the sound of other letters. The letter *c* is hard, as in English 'cat', except when followed by *i* or *e*, when it becomes the soft *ch* of 'cello'. Similarly, *g* is soft (as in the English 'giant') when followed by *i* or *e*–*giardino*, *gelati*; otherwise hard (as in 'gas')–*gatto*. Words ending in *o* are almost always masculine in gender (plural: -*i*); those ending in *a* are generally feminine (plural: -*e*). Use the polite second person (*lei*) to speak to strangers and the informal second person (*tu*) to friends or children.

USEFUL WORDS	
yes	*sì*
no	*no*
please	*per piacere*
thank you	*grazie*
you're welcome	*prego*
excuse me! !	*scusi*
where	*dove*
here	*qui*
there	*là*
when	*quando*
now	*adesso*
later	*più tardi*
why	*perchè*
who	*chi*
may I/can I	*posso*
good morning	*buon giorno*
good afternoon	*buona sera*
good evening	*buona notte*
hello/goodbye (informal)	*ciao*
hello (on the telephone)	*pronto*
I'm sorry	*mi dispiace*
left/right	*sinistra/destra*
open/closed	*aperto/chiuso*
good/bad	*buono/cattivo*
big/small	*grande/piccolo*
with/without	*con/senza*
more/less	*più/meno*
hot/cold	*caldo/freddo*
early/late	*presto/ritardo*
now/later	*adesso/più tardi*
today/tomorrow	*oggi/domani*
when?/do you have?	*quando?/avete?*

NUMBERS	
1	*uno, una*
2	*due*
3	*tre*
4	*quattro*
5	*cinque*
6	*sei*
7	*sette*
8	*otto*
9	*nove*
10	*dieci*
20	*venti*
30	*trenta*
40	*quaranta*
50	*cinquanta*
100	*cento*
1,000	*mille*

EMERGENCIES

help!	aiuto!
stop, thief!	al ladro!
can you help me, please?	può aiutarmi, per favore?
call the police/an ambulance	chiami la polizia/ un'ambulanza
I have lost my wallet/ passport	ho perso il mio portafoglio/il mio passaporto
where is the police station?	dov'è il commissariato?
where is the hospital?	dov'è l'ospedale?
I don't feel well	non mi sento bene
first aid	pronto soccorso

COLOURS

black	nero
brown	marrone
pink	rosa
red	rosso
orange	arancia
yellow	giallo
green	verde
light blue	celeste
sky blue	azzuro
purple	viola
white	bianco
grey	grigio

USEFUL PHRASES

how are you? (informal)	come sta/stai?
I'm fine	sto bene
I do not understand	non ho capito
how much is it?	quant'è?
do you have a room?	avete camere libere?
how much per night?	quanto costa una notte?
with bath/shower	con vasca/doccia
when is breakfast served?	a che ora è servita la colazione?
where is the train/bus station?	dov'è la stazione ferroviaria degli autobus?
where are we?	dove siamo?
do I have to get off here?	devo scendere qui?
I'm looking for...	cerco...
where can I buy...?	dove posso comprare...?
a table for... please	un tavolo per... per favore
the bill, please?	il conto, per favore
we didn't have this	non abbiamo avuto questo
where are the toilets?	dove sono i bagni?

DAYS/MONTHS

Monday	lunedì
Tuesday	martedì
Wednesday	mercoledì
Thursday	giovedì
Friday	venerdì
Saturday	sabato
Sunday	domenica
January	gennaio
February	febbraio
March	marzo
April	aprile
May	maggio
June	giugno
July	luglio
August	agosto
September	settembre
October	ottobre
November	novembre
December	dicembre

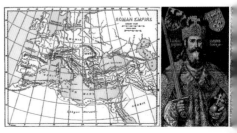

Timeline

PUNIC WARS

The First Punic War against Carthage (North Africa) started in 264BC and lasted for around 23 years. In the Second Punic War (218–201BC) Rome was threatened by Hannibal, leader of the Carthaginian army. But Rome finally defeated Carthage in the Third Punic War (149–146BC).

RELIGION

There are 280 churches within the city walls and 94 per cent of Romans have had their children baptized. However, only 23 per cent of Romans attend Mass. Forty per cent of Romans favour women priests; the same number believe in hell.

Caius Julius Caesar (left)
Map of the Roman Empire (middle)
Charlemagne—his coronation as Holy Roman Emperor (right)

753BC Traditional date of the foundation of Rome by Romulus, first of the city's seven kings.

616–578BC Tarquinius Priscus, Rome's first Etruscan king.

509BC Etruscans expelled and the Republic founded.

60BC Rome ruled by a triumvirate of Pompey, Marcus Licinius Crassus and Julius Caesar.

48BC Caesar declared ruler for life but assassinated by rivals in 44BC.

27BC–AD14 Rule of Octavian, Caesar's great nephew, who as Augustus becomes the first Roman emperor.

98–117 Reign of Emperor Trajan. Military campaigns extend the Empire's boundaries.

284–286 Empire divided into East and West.

306–337 The Emperor Constantine reunites the Empire legalising Christianity. St. Peter's and the first Christian churches are built.

410 Rome is sacked by the Goths.

476 Romulus Augustulus is the last Roman Emperor.

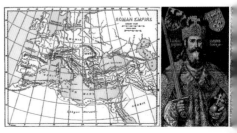

NEED TO KNOW TIMELINE

800 Charlemagne awards some territories to papacy; Pope Leo III crowns him Holy Roman Emperor.

1452–1626 The construction of a new St. Peter's begins and spans over 150 years.

1508 Michelangelo begins the Sistine Chapel ceiling.

1527 Rome is sacked by German and Spanish troops under Charles V.

1848 Uprisings in Rome under Mazzini and Garibaldi force Pope Pius IX to flee. The new 'Roman Republic' is defeated by the French.

1870 Rome joins a united Italy.

1929 The Lateran Treaty recognises the Vatican as a separate state.

1940 Italy enters World War II.

1960 Rome hosts the Olympic Games.

2000 Some 30 million pilgrims visit Rome for the millennial jubilee year.

2005 Pope John Paul II dies and is succeeded by Pope Benedict XVI.

2006 Romano Prodi of the centre left party takes the Italian presidency from Silvio Berlusconi in the April elections.

WHAT'S IN A NAME

Many of Rome's street names include dates that allude to significant events in the city's history. Via XX Settembre (20 September) remembers that day in 1870 when Italian troops liberated Rome: the city became the city's capital in the same year. Via XXIV Maggio (24 May) recalls the day in 1915 that Italy declared war in 1915 during World War I. Via IV Novembre (4 November) alludes to the date of the Italian armistice and victory in 1918 after World War I. And Via XXV Aprile (25 April) commemorates the day in 1944 that the Allies liberated the city from the Nazi rule.

Gladiators at a Funeral (left)
Charlemagne et ses ecoliers (middle)
Garibaldi, a popular leader (right)

Index

INDEX

CITYPACK TOP 25
Rome

WRITTEN BY Tim Jepson
DESIGN CONCEPT AND DESIGN WORK Kate Harling
COVER DESIGN Jackie Bailey
INDEXER Marie Lorimer
IMAGE RETOUCHING AND REPRO Sarah Butler
EDITORIAL MANAGEMENT Apostrophe S Limited
SERIES EDITOR Paul Mitchell

First published 1996
Reprinted September 2008
Colour separation by Keenes
Printed and bound by Leo, China
A CIP catalogue record for this book is available from the British Library.

ISBN 978-0-7495-5250-3

Published by AA Publishing, a trading name of Automobile Association Developments
Limited, whose registered office is Fanum House, Basing View, Basingstoke, Hampshire
RG21 4EA. Registered number 1878835.

A03943
Maps in this title produced from:
  map data © 1998 – 2005 Navigation Technologies BV. All rights reserved.
  with map updates courtesy of MAIRDUMONT, Ostfildern, Germany
  mapping © ISTITUTO GEOGRAFICO DE AGOSTINI S.p.A., NOVARA - 2006
Transport map © Communicarta Ltd, UK

The Automobile Association wishes to thank the following photographers, companies and picture libraries for their assistance in the preparation of this book.

Abbreviations for the picture credits are as follows – (t) top; (b) bottom; (l) left; (r) right; (c) centre; (AA) AA World Travel Library; (F/C) Front Cover; (B/C) Back Cover

F/C AA/C Sawyer; **B/C t** AA/J Holmes; **B/C ct** AA/C Sawyer; **B/C cb** AA/S McBride; **B/C b** AA/S McBride; **1** AA/C Sawyer; **2** AA/A Kouprianoff; **3** AA/A Kouprianoff; **4t** AA/A Kouprianoff; **4c** AA/S McBride; **5t** AA/A Kouprianoff; **5c** AA/D Miterdiri; **6t** AA/A Kouprianoff; **6cl** AA/C Sawyer; **6c** AA/S McBride; **6cr** AA/S McBride; **6bl** AA/C Sawyer; **6cbl** AA/C Sawyer; **6bc** AA/S McBride; **6br** AA/A Kouprianoff; **7t** AA/A Kouprianoff; **7cl** AA/S McBride; **7c** AA/S McBride; **7cr** AA/S McBride; **7bl** AA/S McBride; **7bc** AA/S McBride; **7br** AA/S McBride; **8** AA/A Kouprianoff; **9** AA/A Kouprianoff; **10t** AA/A Kouprianoff; **10ct** AA/S McBride; **10c** AA/S McBride; **10cb** AA/C Sawyer; **10/11** AA/S McBride; **11t** AA/A Kouprianoff; **11ct** AA/C Sawyer; **11c** AA/C Sawyer; **12t** AA/A Kouprianoff; **12b** AA/C Sawyer; **13t** AA/A Kouprianoff; **13tct** AA/A Kouprianoff; **13ct** AA/D Miterdiri; **13c** AA/A Kouprianoff; **13cb** AA; **13b** AA/S McBride; **14t** AA/A Kouprianoff; **14ct** AA/C Sawyer; **14c** AA/J Holmes; **14cb** AA/M Jourdan; **14b** AA/C Sawyer; **15** AA/A Kouprianoff; **16t** AA/A Kouprianoff; **16ct** AA/A Kouprianoff; **16c** AA/C Sawyer; **16cb** AA/A Kouprianoff; **16b** AA/D Miterdiri; **17t** AA/A Kouprianoff; **17ct** Digital Vision; **17c** AA/C Sawyer; **17cb** AA/C Sawyer; **17b** AA/S McBride; **18t** AA/A Kouprianoff; **18ct** AA/P Wilson; **18c** AA/A Kouprianoff; **18cb** AA/C Sawyer; **18b** AA/S McBride; **19i** AA/A Kouprianoff; **19ii** AA/J Holmes; **19iii** AA/J Holmes; **19iv** AA/S McBride; **19v** AA/J Holmes; **19vi** AA/T Souter; **20/21** AA/A Kouprianoff; **24l** AA/J Holmes; **24/25** AA/S McBride; **24c** AA/C Sawyer; **24tr** AA/A Kouprianoff; **24cl** AA/S McBride; **25cr** AA/A Kouprianoff; **26l** AA/A Kouprianoff; **26/27** AA/C Sawyer; **26c** AA/P Wilson; **27c** AA/P Wilson; **27r** AA/S McBride; **28l** AA/S McBride; **28/29** AA/S McBride; **28c** AA/S McBride; **29tr** AA/S McBride; **29cl** AA/S McBride; **29cr** AA/S McBride; **30l** AA/J Holmes; **30r** AA/J Holmes; **31l** AA/S McBride; **31r** AA/M Jourdan; **32l** AA/D Miterdiri; **32r** AA/S McBride; **33t** AA/D Miterdiri; **33bl** AA/T Souter; **33br** AA/S McBride; **34t** AA/D Miterdiri; **34bl** AA/J Holmes; **34br** AA/P Wilson; **35t** AA/D Miterdiri; **35bl** AA/A Kouprianoff; **35br** AA/D Miterdiri; **36** AA/J Holmes; **37t** AA/C Saywer; **37c** AA/S McBride; **38** AA/J Holmes; **39** AA/A Kouprianoff; **40l** Alamy/Pieter Estersohn; **42/43t** AA/S McBride; **42/43b** AA/S McBride; **43** Alamy/CuboImages srl; **44** AA/J Holmes; **44/45** AA/P Wilson; **46l** AA/S McBride; **46tr** AA/S McBride; **46/47** AA/S McBride; **47t** AA/S McBride; **47bl** AA/S McBride; **47br** AA/S McBride; **48l** AA/C Sawyer; **48c** AA/C Sawyer; **48r** AA/C Sawyer; **49l** AA/C Sawyer; **49r** AA/P Wilson; **50l** AA/C Sawyer; **50c** AA; **50r** AA/C Sawyer; **51t** AA/D Miterdiri; **51bl** AA/C Sawyer; **51br** AA/J Holmes; **52t** AA/D Miterdiri; **52bl** AA/D Miterdiri; **52br** AA/J Holmes; **53** AA/D Miterdiri; **54** AA/C Sawyer; **55** AA/P Wilson; **56** AA/C Sawyer; **57** AA/A Kouprianoff; **58** AA/C Sawyer; **59** AA/C Sawyer; **60** AA/C Sawyer; **61** AA/A Kouprianoff; **64l** AA/A Kouprianoff; **64tr** AA/S McBride; **64/65** AA/S McBride; **65t** AA/D Miterdiri; **65cl** AA/S McBride; **65cr** AA/S McBride; **66l** AA/D Miterdiri; **66r** AA/A Kouprianoff; **67t** AA/D Miterdiri; **67bl** AA/S McBride; **67br** AA/S McBride; **68t** AA/D Miterdiri; **68bl** AA/J Holmes; **68br** AA/J Holmes; **69t** AA/D Miterdiri; **69bl** AA/J Holmes; **69br** AA/J Holmes; **70** AA/D Miterdiri; **71** AA/M Chaplow; **72** Digital Vision; **73** Brand X Pictures; **74** AA/T Harris; **75** AA/C Sawyer; **78l** AA/S McBride; **78c** AA/S McBride; **78r** AA/S McBride; **79l** AA/P Wilson; **79r** AA/D Miterdiri; **80l** AA/P Wilson; **80r** AA/P Wilson; **81l** AA/C Sawyer; **81c** AA/J Holmes; **81r** AA/C Sawyer; **82** AA/S McBride; **82/83** Alamy/Rough Guides; **84l** AA/J Holmes; **84r** AA/J Holmes; **85l** AA/D Miterdiri; **85r** Alamy/Peter Horree; **86t** AA/D Miterdiri; **86bl** AA; **86br** AA/D Miterdiri; **87t** AA/D Miterdiri; **87bl** AA/D Miterdiri; **87br** AA/P Wilson; **88** AA/D Miterdiri; **89** Photodisc; **90t** Digital Vision; **90c** AA/E Meacher; **91** AA/J Holmes; **94l** AA/S McBride; **94r** AA/J Holmes; **95l** AA/C Sawyer; **95r** AA/S McBride; **96l** AA/S McBride; **96tr** AA/S McBride; **96cr** AA/S McBride; **97t** AA/S McBride; **97cl** AA/S McBride; **97cr** AA/S McBride; **98t** AA/S McBride; **98c** AA/C Sawyer; **99** AA/S McBride; **102t** AA/S McBride; **102cl** AA/C Sawyer; **102cr** AA/C Saywer; **103t** AA/S McBride; **103cl** AA/C Sawyer; **104t** AA/D Miterdiri; **104bl** AA/S McBride; **104br** AA/J Holmes; **105t** AA/S McBride; **105bl** AA/S McBride; **105bc** AA/S McBride; **105br** AA/S McBride; **106t** Photodisc; **106c** AA/C Sawyer; **107** AA/P Wilson; **108t** AA/C Sawyer; **108ct** Photodisc; **108c** AA/C Sawyer; **108cb** AA/C Sawyer; **108b** AA; **109** AA/C Sawyer; **110** AA/C Sawyer; **111** AA/C Sawyer; **112** AA/C Sawyer; **113** AA/J Holmes; **114** AA/S McBride; **115** AA/S McBride; **116** AA/S McBride; **117** AA/S McBride; **118** AA/S McBride; **119** AA/S McBride; **120** AA/S McBride; **121** AA/S McBride; **122t** AA/S McBride; **122b** AA/J Holmes; **123** AA/S McBride; **124t** AA/S McBride; **124bl** AA; **124bc** AA; **124br** AA; **125t** AA/S McBride; **125bl** AA; **125bc** AA; **125br** AA

Every effort has been made to trace the copyright holders, and we apologise in advance for any unintentional omissions or errors. We would be pleased to apply any corrections in any following edition of this publication.